Praise for It Starts with One

"For any executive this is an excellent roadmap for leading strategic change!"
—Bill Marriott, Chairman and CEO, Marriott International Inc.

"Black and Gregersen debunk the myth that organizations change by changing the organization. They understand the real dynamics a leader must manage to convert the hearts and minds of people in a complex organization to a new direction. If you are trying to shake things up and make lasting change, this is a must-read book."
—Gary L. Crittenden, CFO Citigroup

"All successful businesses accept the need for change. *It Starts with One* steers the reader through the complexities of modern leadership and delivers a powerful framework for transforming old patterns of action into new strategic direction, emphasizing what matters most— the people."
—Edward Dolman, CEO, Christie's International plc

"This book broke my own brain barrier, asking me to think differently about ideas and processes that I'd become too comfortable with. It's a significant contribution to the field of organizational change and will undoubtedly help us be more successful with change. And I love the maps—they provoke my intellect and imagination."
—Margaret J. Wheatley, Author of *Leadership and the New Science*, *Turning to One Another*, and *Finding Our Way*

"What a pleasure to find a book on change focused on 'leading' rather than 'managing' change. Leaders create change; they don't react to it. This book addresses the crux of that leadership issue by focusing on people, where the real change must occur."
—Richard D. Hanks, Chairman and President, Mindshare Technologies

"Finally a book that gets it right. Organizations don't change. People change. *It Starts with One* gives extremely practical tools to make real change happen."
—Jack Zenger, Author of *The Extraordinary Leader* and CEO and Co-founder of Zenger|Folkman

"PROVOCATIVE, PRACTICAL, POWERFUL!"
—Stephen R. Covey, Author of *The Seven Habits of Highly Effective People*

"Few things add greater value than effectively leading strategic change. Few books show you how to do it better than this one."
—Dave Ulrich, Author of *Leadership Brand*, Professor of Business, University of Michigan and Partner, The RBL Group (www.rbl.net)

"A significant barrier to any major change or innovation management process is in transparently defining the past and desired future state, then connecting the move from the former to latter in an inspirational way. *It Starts with One* offers novel framing and straightforward stepback, targeted thinking that can streamline and turbocharge the challenging change process."

—David N. DiGiulio, Consultant and former Vice President, Research & Development, Procter & Gamble

"Leading successful strategic change is one of the biggest and most important challenges executives face today. Black and Gregersen offer a practical set of concepts and tools to meet that challenge."

—Sue Lee, Senior Vice President, Human Resources and Communications, Suncor Energy Inc.

"I found this book special in several ways. It is not the usual description of the stages of change. Instead, it describes the process of change in human terms—the way people really experience it. They go beneath and look at assumptions (mind maps) that hold people back from being able to change."

—Jean Broom, Consultant and former Senior Vice President, Human Resources, Itochu International, Inc.

"Talk about change has far outstripped leaders' ability to successfully lead it. Black and Gregersen push the change leaders to explore how they think about or 'map' the world in which we live. These maps become either a critical barrier or an asset to their ability to lead change. The authors also provide a challenging self-examination for the serious leader to assess his or her ability to create long-lasting and effective change. Thoughtful leaders will give this a very thoughtful read."

—Ralph Christensen, Author of *Roadmap to Strategic HR*

"Strategic change happens one person at a time. Black and Gregersen bring this statement to life by supplying critical insight combined with essential tools for helping individuals negotiate their way through organizational change."

—Tyler Bolli, Director, Human Resources, Kohler Company

"This book presents a refreshing new way to think about leading change in organizations. Black and Gregersen redraw our maps of the change process in a compelling and practical way that gets right to the heart of making real change possible."

—Marion Shumway, Organization Development Program Manager, Intel

"Insightful handbook packed full of valuable wisdom for unlocking the power of mental maps in any organization's change efforts."
—**Dave Kinard, Executive Director for Leadership and Organizational Development, Eli Lilly and Company**

"Too often in the trenches of organizational life, we deceive ourselves by believing that if we get the boxes in an organization chart or the big systems behind the boxes just right, then organizations change. Black and Gregersen artfully uncover this deception by revealing a new, eye-opening approach to change that can help any leader of change become much stronger and better at it."
—**Mark Hamberlin, Director, Human Resources European Markets Cisco Systems Inc.**

IT STARTS
STARTS
with ONE

IT
STARTS
with ONE

CHANGING INDIVIDUALS CHANGES ORGANIZATIONS

SECOND EDITION

J. STEWART BLACK, INSEAD
HAL B GREGERSEN, INSEAD

Vice President, Editor-in-Chief: Tim Moore
Associate Publisher and Director of Marketing: Amy Neidlinger
Wharton Editor: Yoram (Jerry) Wind
Acquisitions Editor: Martha Cooley
Editorial Assistant: Pamela Boland
Development Editor: Russ Hall
Digital Marketing Manager: Julie Phifer
Marketing Coordinator: Megan Colvin
Cover Designer: Chuti Prasertsith
Managing Editor: Gina Kanouse
Senior Project Editor: Kristy Hart
Copy Editor: Lisa Thibault
Indexer: Erika Millen
Senior Compositor: Gloria Schurick
Manufacturing Buyer: Dan Uhrig

© 2008 by Pearson Education, Inc.
Publishing as Wharton School Publishing
Upper Saddle River, New Jersey 07458

Wharton School Publishing offers excellent discounts on this book
when ordered in quantity for bulk purchases or special sales.
For more information, please contact U.S. Corporate and Government Sales, 1-800-
382-3419, corpsales@pearsontechgroup.com. For sales outside the U.S., please
contact International Sales at international@pearsoned.com.

Printed in the United States of America

Sections of the work previously appeared in 2003.

Second Printing April 2008

ISBN 10: 0-13-231984-5
ISBN 13: 978-0-13-231984-3

Pearson Education LTD.
Pearson Education Australia PTY, Limited.
Pearson Education Singapore, Pte. Ltd.
Pearson Education North Asia, Ltd.
Pearson Education Canada, Ltd.
Pearson Educatio[ac]n de Mexico, S.A. de C.V.
Pearson Education—Japan
Pearson Education Malaysia, Pte. Ltd.

Library of Congress Cataloging-in-Publication Data

Black, J. Stewart, 1959-

It starts with one : changing individuals changes organizations / J. Stewart Black,
Hal B. Gregersen. — 2nd ed.

p. cm.

Rev. ed. of: Leading strategic change. c2002.

ISBN 0-13-231984-5 (hardback : alk. paper) 1. Organizational change—Planning. 2.
Group decision making. I. Gregersen, Hal B., 1958- II. Black, J. Stewart, 1959-
Leading strategic change. III. Title.

HD58.8.B547 2008
658.4'02—dc22

2007014700

Dedicated to our mothers

Contents

Acknowledgments

The premise of this book is that large-scale change rests on the ability to change individuals. In our experience, few people have done that better than our professor, mentor, and friend, J. Bonner Ritchie. When we were students at Brigham Young University more than 20 years ago, we had the privilege of learning from one of the great master teachers, who, through his questions and examples, inspired change in ourselves and other individual students over the years beyond what we had seen before or have seen since.

Bonner was a champion of change, whether as a student at the University of California, Berkeley, an officer in the U.S. Army, a faculty member and civil rights activist at The University of Michigan, a business consultant to African-American catfish farmers, a chairperson of the Utah State Liquor Commission, a professor at Brigham Young University, or as a tireless advocate of peace and prosperity for children around the world. Among other things, when we were students Bonner showed us the power of maps and metaphors and their ability to help us see things both differently and more clearly. As you read this book, on this issue you will see his hand in every chapter.

Along with Bonner, many other colleagues have contributed to the shaping of our thinking about change in general and the ideas in this book specifically. Thanks to Jean Broom, Mark Hamberlin, Spencer Harrison, Paul McKinnon, Mark Mendenhall, Allen Morrison, Gary Oddou, Lee Perry, Lyman Porter, Kurt Sandholtz, Marion Shumway, Greg Stewart, Pat Stocker, Michael Thompson, Dave Ulrich, and Dave Whetten. In addition, we are appreciative of the thousands of executives and hundreds of students at Brigham Young University, Dartmouth College, The University of Michigan, Helsinki School of Economics, Pennsylvania State University, and INSEAD who have engaged in learning with us and helped us sharpen our thoughts and insights.

On the home front, our respective parents played pivotal roles, not only in forming our maps of the world, but also in teaching us how to create new maps. We are grateful for the gifts of inquiry that our parents passed on. We also thank each of our children—Jared, Nathaniel, Kendra, Ian, and Devyn from the Black family, as well as Kancie, Matt, Emilee, Ryan, Kourtnie, Amber, and Jordon from the Schaefer Gregersen family—for enduring our quirky mental maps and helping rewrite and update tired and well-worn ones that needed radical change. Finally, to our respective wives—Tanya Maria Black and Suzi Gregersen—we are forever grateful for your efforts in helping us navigate through this adventurous treasure map of life.

J. Stewart Black
Hal B Gregersen

About the Authors

J. Stewart Black is a professor at INSEAD, the oldest and largest MBA program in Europe. An internationally recognized scholar on change and transformation, he is a frequent keynote speaker at conferences around the world and company functions. He is regularly sought out to work with leading companies on issues of strategy and strategic change, especially with regard to developing leaders and high-potential managers to initiate and execute change in themselves and others. Dr. Black has been a faculty member previously at the Amos Tuck School of Business Administration at Dartmouth College and The University of Michigan. He is the author of 10 other books and more than 100 articles and case studies that have been used in both university classrooms and corporate boardrooms. Dr. Black has lived, worked, and spent significant time in many countries including, Japan, Singapore, Hong Kong, and France.

Hal B Gregersen is a professor of leadership at INSEAD where he delivers world-class research ideas on leading strategic change and innovation to executives from every continent. He regularly consults with senior teams, conducts executive seminars, and delivers keynote speeches on innovation and change in companies such as Christie's, Daimler, IBM, Intel, Johnson & Johnson, LG, Marriott International, Nokia, Sun Microsystems, and Yahoo. Before joining INSEAD, Dr. Gregersen was a faculty member at the London Business School, the Tuck School of Business Administration at Dartmouth College, Brigham Young University, and Helsinki School of Economics, as well as a Fulbright Fellow at the Turku School of Economics. He has co-authored 9 other books and more than 90 articles and cases on leading innovation and change that have also been highlighted on CNN and in *Business Week, Fortune, Psychology Today*, and *The Wall Street Journal*. Dr. Gregersen calls Finland,

France, and the U.S. his homes, having lived in all three countries. He also travels the world, camera in hand (a passionate avocation), photographing diverse people and places to foster deeper insight into the dynamics of innovation and change.

Foreword

by Stephen R. Covey

Oliver Wendell Holmes emphasized, "I wouldn't give a fig for the simplicity on this side of complexity, but I would give my right arm for the simplicity on the far side of complexity." This book is "simplicity on the far side of complexity." Using the Pareto Principle, where 80 percent of the desired results flow from 20 percent of activities, Stewart Black and Hal Gregersen have put a laser beam focus on that 20 percent. They effectively get at the subtle the important dynamics and practical solutions involved in bringing about change in our highly accelerated, complex, globalized world.

I have many friends and associates in the strategy and consulting world, and it has almost become a joke that in spite of brilliant analytical studies of the opportunities and threats inside an industry or a profession, in spite of extensive research into alternative strategies, in spite of brilliant feasibility studies and recommended strategic paths, seldom are these strategies effectively *implemented*. This is particularly true in today's digital, globalized world, simply because the hearts and minds of the people—the culture, if you will—are too mired in the past and people fail "to see" the need for change. They thereby fail to cultivate the new skill set and to organize the resources "to move" forward and "to finish" the job.

The logic of this book is compellingly built around a paradigm or mental map of inside-out (individual out) rather than outside-in (organization in). Unless the needed change is embedded in individuals, it cannot show up in the larger organization in a way that consistently affects behavior and results. It reminds me of a statement that the great sociologist Emile Durkheim said: "When mores are sufficient, laws are unnecessary. When mores are insufficient, laws are unenforceable." In other words, when looking at the issue of organizational change, until the needed changes get deeply embedded in the values, mindset, and skill set of individuals, organization change simply will not happen—no matter how brilliant the new organizational strategy, structure, or systems. As the subtitle of the book says, "changing individuals changes organizations," not the other way around.

I remember a visit I had with the president of Toyota in Japan. He was talking about the cultivation of the spirit of "kaisen," meaning "continuous improvement." He emphasized how absolutely necessary it was for the hearts and minds of the people "on the line," to emotionally connect with kaisen, to deeply "see" or buy into it as informed, economically literate and involved people. In fact, he even suggested that the level of this understanding and involvement should reach the point that every _one_ desires and takes responsibility to make things better and any one individual can stop the line and initiate a discussion on how to make things better, improve quality, and lower costs. I remember him saying, "Detroit simply doesn't get it. They think the answer is in marketing and design and technique and technology. They don't understand that the answer lies in the hearts and minds of every individual worker." In other words, using the language of Stewart and Hal's mentor and my dear friend, J. Bonner Ritchie, the Toyota workers had their own "map," consequently their own "metaphor," to guide their behavior

Of course, deep change does not happen instantly. To some, this approach may seem less efficient, but after more than 40 years of experience, I can say with confidence that the approach is infinitely more effective. Why is this more important today than ever before? Simply because we are moving out of the Industrial Age into the Knowledge Worker Age. Today 70–80 percent of the value added to goods and services comes from knowledge work, where even 20-30 years ago it was only 20–30 percent. The job of leadership in the Industrial Age was one of control, rather than one of unleashing human talent. People became cost centers and were managed like things; just like machinery, to be controlled.

But because unlike machinery people had feelings, and getting different behavior out of them required more than simply adjusting a knob or dial. As a consequence, the carrot-and-stick—the Great Jackass Theory of Human Motivation—became the dominant change tool during this era.

Thankfully the world has changed. Today managers recognize that people have minds and hearts and spirits, not just bodies to be controlled and manipulated. People today want a sense of meaning, a sense of voice, a sense of belonging to an innovative community that adds true value. It is a different world, and the need for changing to that different world, as well as transforming how we bring about change in others, has become compellingly clear and obvious. Paraphrasing the great historian Arnold Toynbee, "You can summarize the history of organizations, institutions and societies in four simple worlds: 'Nothing fails like success.'" In other words, if you have a new challenge, the old successful response routinely fails. Thus it is with organizations: The old successful carrot-and-stick way of bringing about change fails in our new environment. To become competitive at a world-class level today and into the future, change must be anticipatory change, not reactive change, or change because of crisis, as this book so compellingly illustrates. However, despite the ever-larger size of organizations, with ones like Wal-Mart likely to have 2 million employees around the world within a decade, the reality is that leaders must keep individuals at the center of the change process. Mother Theresa once said, "If I look at the mass, I will never act. If I look at the one, I will."

From my own work with organizations, I have learned that the key to the 99 is the one, and also that every one of the 99 *is* one. I have also learned the central lesson taught in this book is that until individuals deeply see and feel the need for change, make the necessary moves, and fight to the finish in making good things happen, the change will not work its way into the culture (the shared value systems of individuals), and until that happens you simply don't see sustained change with powerful positive impacts.

I have seldom seen a work so replete with such powerful, real-life business examples that readers can relate to. These are not abstract examples, but compelling real-life examples of businesses that most of us have done business with, either through our businesses or as consumers. As the book clearly illustrates, we need a new mental model or map, regarding the very processes of change itself, so we don't fall back into the Industrial Age model of control and manipulation. We have to get past the notion that changing organization strategies, structures, or systems will magically change individuals. This last mindset change is the toughest of all. In science this is called a *paradigm shift*. From a historical review of these shifts, we know they are not easy because every significant scientific breakthrough has required a "break with" an old way of thinking, an old paradigm, an old model, an old map. Ptolemy, the Egyptian astrologist, developed the map that the Earth is the center of the universe. It was not only Earth-centric, it was egocentric. Copernicus showed that the Earth revolves around the sun and that the sun is the center of our universe, and that there are many universes. He was castigated as a heretic. Such a flawed map persisted for centuries. Even Galileo, many centuries later, proved through the telescope the Copernican model correct, and he himself was castigated as a heretic, put out in front of a church and every parishioner stepped on his body. At the end, he lifts his bloody body and head and they asked him, "What do you have to say now?" and he says, "The earth still revolves."

Bloodletting was the common medical practice for much of the Middle Ages, even after the Germ Theory had been discovered by Semmelweis out of Hungary and Pasteur out of France. The Divine Right of Kings paradigm persisted for millennia. Then the concept of "government of the people, by the people, for the people," surfaced to unleash the greatest prosperity known to man, a profound breakthrough.

In 2006, Mohammed Yunus received the Nobel Peace Prze for his leadership of the worldwide micro-credit movement, wherein less than a generation of more than 500 million people have come out of poverty. What was the key? A new map that viewed people as able and responsible and saw that in aggregate many seemingly small changes could result in a great movement. One of the keys in creating a culture where people who received credit paid it back was that the women who received credit sat on the credit committee to evaluate the next applicant. A deep change in individuals became embedded into the culture of many. The fundamental value was that if you receive credit, you pay back. The result was an astounding 98.9 percent payback. Armed with new paradigms, you can see why Leonard E. Read's statement, "Every significant movement in history has been led by one or just a few individuals with a small minority of energetic supporters" is so true.

Robert Peel, the founder of modern policing, put it this way: "The basic mission of police is to PREVENT crime and disorder. The public are the police and the police are the public, and both share the same responsibility for community safety." This is a new map. This is a map of prevention rather than just catching bad guys. Today community policing has become the most powerful force in preventing crime. Because it involves tapping into individuals, parents, children, and teenagers, in many places in the world today, crime has been reduced up to 80 percent, and recidivism has gone down to 5 percent. So many other illustrations from different fields of human endeavor could be shown to demonstrate that "every significant breakthrough for the future is a break with the past."

Bottom line, this book is a breakthrough book because it is a break with the outside-in approach to change and gives innumerable practical frameworks of thinking and illustrations. The authors demonstrate the need for a new change process, inside-out, based on the idea that until the heart and mind of an individual change, not much else will happen. Simply announcing a new strategy or structure will not do much, even if the announcement is communicated by videocast, podcast, webcast, satellite, cable, microwave, or any other broadcast. Why? Execution will not happen. On average, only about one-third of people say they clearly understand what their organizations are trying to achieve, and only 10 percent feel very highly energized by and committed to their organization's goals. Why? Because trying to impose change from the organization onto the individual doesn't work in a more global and sophisticated world. You have to work from the inside out.

At first this may seem like a significant and perhaps overwhelming demand, especially if you are a senior executive with ultimate responsibility over hundreds, or thousands—or hundreds of thousands—of employees. Along with the authors, I look at it differently. It is not only possible but vastly more rewarding to help individuals see the need for a change, empower them to make the necessary moves, and encourage and support them through the finish. In turn, they can then repeat the same rewarding personal change process throughout their lives. We are capable of it. We have the power of choice. We are the creative force of our own lives. We can lift ourselves out of the quicksand of past habits, past practices, however successful they may have been, and can rise to this new world challenge and the magnificent new opportunities that it provides. But it all starts with one. It starts with each one of us and our relationships with one another.

Perhaps Margaret Mead put it best: "Never doubt that a small group of committed people can change the world; indeed, it is the only thing that ever has."

Preface

Few will dispute that we currently face one of the greatest challenges and opportunities in modern history. As we navigate the waters of modern business, we do so at a time when even the most seasoned and experienced executives and companies are reeling from the powerful and somewhat unpredictable winds, tides, and waves of globalization. This churning environment can provide the chance for some to rise to new heights while sending others to the bottom of the sea. For example, we live in a world where a company that didn't even exist when we sent the first edition of this book to the publisher in 2002—Wikipedia—emerged to create three times the content of *Encyclopedia Britannica*, the original industry creator and benchmark company for more than 250 years.

Thus, it is not into calm waters that we sail, but into a tumultuous sea of opportunity and risk. As we enter this future, government and business executives will face nearly a constant sea of change—changes in technology, society, demographics, competitors, suppliers, and so on. Change of any significance has never been easy, and in the turbulent world of the future we can expect it to be even more challenging. Perhaps this is why between 50–70 percent of all strategic change initiatives fail. With such a high average failure rate, the difference between successful companies and executives will largely rest on those who can effectively implement change and those who cannot.

This book is about that process. We start by outlining why most change initiatives fail, and then describe what we can do to avoid common pitfalls and ultimately succeed at leading strategic change. Based on our research and experience, it turns out that the key to successful change is not systems such as information, pay, or communication, but at the core it's people. If you cannot get the people to see the need for change, to make the needed changes, and to follow through, all the time and money spent on information systems, pay systems, communication systems, or new organizational structures is wasted.

This is why we believe this book delivers unique value to executives and managers. Today more than ever before, people are a company's greatest resource, and they are key to sustainable competitive advantage. However, the constantly changing nature of the world means that executives cannot simply set their people off in one direction doing things a certain way and then put their organization on auto-pilot. A new technology, competitor, government regulation, or other innovation can easily make what was right for today incredibly wrong for tomorrow. If executives and managers can more effectively help people see the need for changes, provide the resources to make the changes, and follow up and reinforce the changes, then the people will propel the company forward. If not, the reality of the future will fall far short of the promised vision.

The world stands at one of the greatest moments in history, at the beginning of an upcoming century of breathtaking change. In 100 years, when we look back at the successes and failures, we believe that much of the success and failure will have been determined by those who were—or were not—capable of leading strategic change. We hope in some small way that this book will have been an influence for good in helping executives and managers become better leaders of change at work and in the world.

The Challenge of Leading Strategic Change

With more than a hundred books on leading strategic change to choose from, why read this one? The answer is simple. Most other books on change have it backwards. They take an "organization in" approach; in other words, they outline all the organizational levers you should pull to change the company based on the premise that if you change the organization, individual change will follow. Our experience and research commands the opposite conclusion. Lasting success lies in changing individuals first; then the organization follows. This is because an organization changes only as far or as fast as its collective individuals change. Without individual change, there is no organizational change. Consequently, instead of an "organization in" approach, we take an "individual out" approach. To repeat—to change your organization, you must *first* change individuals, and sometimes (maybe even often) this means changing yourself as well.

Let's assume for a moment that you agree with this first premise and believe that simply changing some organizational features such as structure will **not** necessarily cause people to change their behaviors. Let's assume that you believe that in order to change an organization, you have to first change the mindset and behaviors of individuals. Even then you still might be wondering, "How difficult can changing individuals be?" Based on our research and experience throughout the last 20 years with nearly 10,000 managers, the failure rate for change initiatives is high—close to 80 percent! When we cite this figure, many managers' reaction is to say, "That sounds a bit high." However, if you put this in an everyday context, the failure rate is not that surprising. For example, of the people who determine to change their diet or level of exercise, how many are still sticking with the change just three weeks later? It is only about 10–15 percent. If people cannot easily and successfully change their own behavior when they say they want to, why would we be surprised that people have about the same level of difficulty and failure changing the behavior of others when the other person may not want to change?

But let's not quibble about numbers. Other studies suggest that the percentage of change failure is only 50 percent. But whether it is 50 or 80 percent, it is not 30 percent. This is significant, because if the failure rate were 30 percent, we might attribute it to the failings of less motivated and skilled managers. But at 50–80 percent, this means that we have many motivated, skilled, and otherwise successful leaders who are nonetheless falling short of their organizational, unit, team, or individual change objectives.

This brings us to some inconvenient truths about change. First, while we would like change to be easy, the inconvenient truth is that it is hard. Second, while we might wish for change to be inexpensive and not require much time, money, effort, blood, sweat, or tears, the inconvenient truth is that change is very expensive. Third, while we might pray for change to be over in a flash, the inconvenient truth is that it often takes a significant amount of time for a change to take hold.

This is why elevating and enhancing the capability of leading change is one of the most profitable things you can do for your career and for your company. In our research, a little more than 80 percent of companies listed leading change as one of the top five core leadership competencies for the future. Perhaps more importantly, 85 percent felt that this competency was not as strong as was needed within their high potential leaders. In a nutshell, when it comes to leading change, demand is high (and growing), and supply is short.

To understand why there is a shortage of capable leaders of change, we only need to consider a few factors. First, change has **never** been easy. For example, consider this quote written 500 years ago by Niccolo Machiavelli:

There is nothing more difficult to carry out, nor more doubtful of success, nor more dangerous to handle than to initiate a new order of things. For the reformer has enemies in all those who profit by the old order, and only lukewarm defenders by all those who could profit by the new order. This lukewarmness arises from the incredulity of mankind who *do not truly believe in anything new until they have had actual experience with it.*

Clearly, resistance to change is not a modern phenomenon. In fact, resistance to change seems to have endured through the ages in part because humans are biologically hardwired to resist change. Yes, that's right. We are programmed *not* to change. While plants may evolve and survive through random variation and natural selection, man does not. We do not generate random variations in behavior and let nature take its course—selecting and de-selecting those that fit and do not fit the environment. Humans are wired to resist random change and thereby avoid random de-selection. We are wired to survive, so we hang on to what has worked in the past. We hang on to successful past "mental maps" and use them to guide current and future behavior.

This map-clinging dynamic happened to Hal a few years ago when he was teaching in the Amos Tuck School of Business at Dartmouth College. Even though Hal only lived about a mile from work and had several possible ways to get there, he had quickly settled in on a habitual driving route that took him to work the fastest. One cold winter morning, though, Hal had driven about halfway to work when he confronted a detour barricade and sign. Construction workers were laying new pipe under the road, and it was clear this was a major project and was going to take a few days, so Hal had to turn around, backtrack halfway home, and then follow a detour route to work. At the end of the workday, Hal began his short drive home. But again, he took his "usual" route and ended up stuck at the detour sign once more. He backed up (just like he did in the morning) and ultimately rerouted himself home. The next day Hal woke up and hurried off to work, and you guessed it. He took his "usual" route again and ended up staring once more at the detour sign. Like the day before, he turned around, backtracked, followed the detour route, and made it to work. Finally, on the afternoon of the second day, Hal altered his mental map of how to drive home and actually rerouted himself *before* running into the detour sign.

Unfortunately, modern times have conspired to work against this ancient biological coding of hanging on to what works until undeniable evidence mounts to prove that the old map no longer fits the new environment. Today, the rate and magnitude of required change has grown exponentially. We now talk about 90-day years (or Internet years, which are almost as short as dog years.) Pundits pull out charts and statistics about the half-life of products dropping in half. Many of us face change of such size, scope, and complexity that is nearly overwhelming. Sadly, all indications are that things are only going to get worse. Specifically, the magnitude of change, rate of change, and unpredictability of change all seem to be headed in the direction of making leading change an ever more challenging leadership capability.

Magnitude of Change

The magnitude and size of the changes we face and will face are Everest in nature. For example, who could have imagined in early 2004 that later that year a company virtually unknown outside of China (Lenovo) would buy the PC business of IBM? In capital terms (at $1.25 billion), it may not have been the biggest acquisition for the year, but in terms of the news splash it was enormous in size. In the same vein, but on an even bigger scale, who in early 2005 would have predicted that CNOOC (Chinese National Offshore Oil Company) would have launched but then lost an $18.5 billion bid for Unocal?

We draw the Lenovo and CNOOC examples from China not because China is the only big change in recent times, but because it is a great example of the size of changes we are experiencing. For example, from 2000 to 2006, not only did foreign direct investment in China more than double to more than $65 billion, but China sucked in nearly 9 out of every 10 foreign dollars, euro, or yen that were invested in all of Asia. In late 2006, the largest IPO ever occurred when Industrial and Commercial Bank of China (ICBC) simultaneously listed its shares on the Shanghai and Hong Kong stock exchanges and pulled in $20 billion! In fact, in 2006, China was the largest IPO market in the world.

As we said, while China is not the only big change out there, it does illustrate the size of changes that have happened recently and will likely happen in the future. China's rise has rippled through all sorts of sectors, including ones that may not get the press that ICBC's IPO did. For example, the large shipment of goods from China to the U.S. but the relatively smaller amounts shipped from the U.S. to China has spawned a new business in California—container storage. There are so many empty containers piling up in California that real estate agents and landowners are making good money simply storing the empty containers on vacant land. In fact, in some cases, the containers are stacked so high that they block the views of homeowners living next to these "temporary" storage facilities.

India may be next in line to send change tectonic tremors throughout the world. While FDI in India in 2006 was only a bit larger than $4 billion compared to more than $65 billion for China, one need look no further than companies such as Infosys, Wipro, Tata, or Reliance for future (some would say current) global competitors. In terms of opportunities, India's middle class, estimated at 250 million people, may offer the foundation upon which to build homegrown multinationals as well as a significant opportunity for growth for foreign multinationals. What will happen in India or how India might affect the global business landscape is nearly impossible to predict, but the magnitude of the potential impact should not be underestimated. Summarized simply, Nandan Nilekani, the CEO of Infosys, recently stated, "We changed the rules of the game…(and) you cannot wish away this new era of globalization."[1] Wen Jiabo, the Chinese prime minister, framed the point even more powerfully: "India and China can together reshape the world order."[2]

Rate of Change

If these and other changes would just come at us at a slow enough rate, like eating an elephant over a long enough period of time, we could digest them one large bit at a time. Unfortunately, the gods of the change universe are not so kind or considerate. Instead, both the rate of change within sectors, as well as across sectors, seems to be accelerating.

Consider that the first significant mention of VOIP (Voice Over Internet Protocol) in Fortune magazine was in 2000. Just three years later in 2003, a small company called Skype was started. One year later in 2004, Fortune magazine told us not to believe all the hype about VOIP. One year after that in 2005 (just two years after its founding), Skype had 53 million customers, and at any given moment Skype had more than 2 million customers using the service and calling friends, family, and loved ones all across the globe at 2 to 7 cents a minute. Later that

[1] Friedman, T. L. "Small and Smaller," New York Times, April 3, 2004.
[2] Kabir, M. A. "Present caretaker government and relevant issues," March 23, 2007, http://www.weeklyholiday.net/2007/230307/com.html.

year in September 2005, eBay bought Skype in a deal that could bring
$4 billion to Skype. From zero to 53 million customers, from zero value
to $4 billion in two years! From just about any perspective, that is fast.
Arguably, it is this fast pace of change that was just too much for AT&T,
the "mother of all bells," and contributed to its being bought out in
2005 for $16.9 billion by SBC, one of the "baby bells" it gave birth to in
1984. Imagine, the 25-year-old child bought out the 135-year-old parent!
(However, to keep it all in the family, SBC adopted and now goes by the
AT&T name.)

Unpredictability of Change

As should be evident from the previous examples on the magnitude and
rate of change, many of the biggest and quickest changes have also been
hard to predict. Would fortune tellers have done any worse job predicting
the rise of VOIP than *Fortune* (or any other magazine) did? We doubt it.
To be clear, we are not picking on *Fortune*; it's a great organization and
produces a quality product; this is why it is one of the most widely read
and quoted magazines. But that is exactly our point. If the best business
journalists talking with the best business minds can't get the future right,
then it just reinforces how unpredictable the future is.

As a last example of the unpredictability of change, consider the rise and
fall of *Encyclopedia Britannica*. Arguably, *Encyclopedia Britannica*
invented the category in which it competes. The first edition was
published progressively from 1768 to 1771 as *Encyclopædia Britannica*.
When it was completed, it contained 2,391 pages and 160 engraved
illustrations in 3 volumes. For more than 200 years, it dominated the
category it created. It was considered the most authoritative encyclopedia
in the market. By the third edition, published 1788–97, it contained
18 volumes plus a 2-volume supplement of more than 16,000 pages.

After the 11th edition (often called the 1911 edition), the trademark and
publication rights were sold to Sears Roebuck of Chicago, Illinois.
Thirty years later, Sears Roebuck offered the rights to the University of
Chicago. From then until his death in 1973, William Benton served as
the publisher.

For the next decade, Britannica continued to dominate the market. A
full set was priced at between $1,500 to $2,000. Then in the mid-1980s
a little known company called Microsoft (only 10 years of age)
approached Britannica Inc. to discuss a potential collaboration.

Britannica turned them down flat. Why would a company with such a stellar brand and reputation that had been successful for more than 200 years team up with a new and unknown company in general, and one that had no place or standing in the publishing world specifically? Rebuffed, Microsoft used content from *Funk & Wagnalls Standard Encyclopedia* to create what is now known as Encarta. Executives at Britannica could only smile as desperation drove one of its more lowly esteemed competitors into the arms of such a strange and immature bedfellow as Microsoft. This view was only reinforced by the growing sales at Britannica during the next five years, hitting $650 million in 1990.

Just three years later in 1993, Microsoft began bundling *Encarta* with its MS Office suite of products. While Encarta's content was not nearly as good as Britannica's, it was essentially free. Britannica's sale dropped like a rock. Determined to survive, Britannica came out with a CD-ROM version, but all the information could not fit on one disk. It came on three disks, making it inconvenient for customers because depending on what information you wanted you had to make sure you put in the correct disk. On top of that, Britannica priced its CD offering at $995. The hope was that such a high price for three CDs would encourage customers to stay with the nicely bound volumes. The plan did not work, and in 1994, Britannica launched an online version of its famed encyclopedia. However, the cost of a subscription was $2,000. Again, the hope was that such a high-priced online subscription would encourage customers to stay with the nicely bound, traditional book sets.

Sales plummeted yet further. In 1996, only 20,000 hard copy versions were sold compared with 117,000 in 1990. Owing to its financial difficulties, in 1996, financier Jacob Safra bought Britannica Inc. for $135 million, a fraction of its book value.

Up to this point, the tale of Britannica is a sad one. The size of the change (Britannica shrank by more than an 80 percent) and speed of the change (it happened in just 2 percent of the company's life span), were both dramatic. However, in the end Britannica's fate was sealed not by Microsoft, but by a company that didn't exist nor was its existence even possible in 1996 when Jacob Safra swooped in to try and save Britannica. That company is Wikipedia. In fact, the ironic point of this tale is that virtually all the information we have conveyed about Encyclopedia Britannica can be found at www.wikipedia.com—a free, online, and "open source" encyclopedia that relies on literally tens of thousands of contributors. Neither Britannica nor Microsoft envisioned this form of encyclopedia in 2001, the year Wikipedia got going. Even as recently as 2003, no one predicted that by 2007, Wikipedia would have 1.5 million articles in English totaling more than 500 million words. To put this in perspective, this makes it three times larger than the largest *Encyclopedia Britannica* set. Who could have seen a pace of change so fast that, in just a few short years, Wikipedia would have 4.6 million articles consisting of 1.4 billion words across 200 languages? In fact, the speed at which Wikipedia is being updated is so fast that even if you read all the new and edited material seven days a week, 24 hours a day, you could not keep up.

Implications of Change

The bottom line is that the size, speed, and unpredictability of change are greater than ever before. Whether there are ten forces flattening the world, or seven drivers of a borderless business environment, or five mega-trends, the fact remains that the challenge of change is here to stay and is only going to get more daunting. Consequently, the costs of being late with change can be not just inconvenient but devastating.

We don't have to look far to see the consequences of not meeting this challenge. AT&T, GM, Kmart, Kodak, and Xerox, in the U.S.; ABB, Airbus, and De Beers in Europe; and Mitsubishi and Sony in Japan, are just a few examples of companies that faltered, brought in new leaders to champion change, and still failed to recover. Any of these companies may yet recover and revitalize just as IBM or Nissan did (at least for a decade). However, the cost of recovering from crisis in terms of lost shareholder value, reputation, or jobs for employees are inevitably higher than if the companies and their leaders had met the challenge of change earlier.

However, the challenge of change is not confined to the boardroom. In fact, in our experience the real battles happen below the radar screen of newspaper and magazine headlines. The reality is that for every failed change featured in some headline, there are literally hundreds of failures far below the CEO suite. These seemingly invisible individual examples consist of innumerable upper- and middle-level leaders whose seemingly fast-track careers were derailed when a change initiative they were leading crashed and burned.

For those whose careers or reputations have not been tarnished by a failed change initiative, the frustrating but inescapable fact of the matter seems to be that no matter how good we have been at leading change in the past, the future will demand even more of us. Therefore, our view is that past success, even for a given individual manager, is not a good predictor of future performance when it comes to leading change. The specific changes any one of us might be called upon to lead are as varied as the industries, countries, and companies we work in. The change might involve:

- Transforming a business unit that succeeded for years by focusing on technological prowess into a unit that must now focus on customer service.
- Leading an organization from domestic competition onto the global battlefield.
- Accelerating growth by focusing not just on building things, but on all the services that go with after-sales support.
- Changing the culture from one of considered deliberations to fast, first-moving decision-makers.
- Redesigning jobs to incorporate new technology that we hardly understand.
- Changing our personal leadership style from a command and control focus to one that is more network-centric and inclusive.
- Something else equally daunting.

In looking at these and myriad other changes, we have observed an important but often overlooked fact for leaders. It is this: Rarely, if ever, are changes required of an organization, a business, a unit, or a team that require no change from the one leading that organization, business, unit, or team. In fact, quite often when we survey or interview those whom the leaders view as needing to change, their comment is, "I hear what my leader is saying, but I'm watching what he or she is doing." In other words, in many cases, those whom the leader is trying to influence and change are looking up but often see no change in the leader. In effect, to them the leader is saying, "Do as I say, not as I do." Sometimes it seems that we have forgotten that this approach never worked for our parents when we were children, nor does it work for us as parents. The principle of "leading by example" is true enough that the approach of "do as I say, not as I do" does not work for anyone— neither as parents nor as leaders.

As a consequence, our experience is that the most successful leaders of change not only recognize that organizational change requires first changing individuals, but that changing other individuals first requires leading by example and changing oneself.

Unfortunately, most people (ourselves included) are programmed to resist change. For example, try this simple experiment. Ask two people to stand face to face and then raise their arms to shoulder height, palms forward. Then request each person to press their palm against that of the other person standing opposite them. What happens? As soon as you feel pressure coming from the other person into your hands, you resist. It is almost a reflex reaction. So it is with change. As soon as people (again including ourselves) feel some pressure, almost instinctively we push back; we resist. Not only that, but the harder people are pushed to change, it seems the more forcefully they resist. It is almost as if they are unconscious disciples of Newtonian physics and automatically feel obliged that for every action to change them they must exhibit an equal and opposite reaction to resist.

As we briefly mentioned earlier, we all have mental maps, and the more these maps have worked in the past, the more deeply entrenched they are in our brains. By the way, this is nearly a literal expression. That is, as impulses travel over the same neural pathways, they etch the path ever deeper in our brains. Efforts to redraw and change mental maps and walk in new paths are almost always met with resistance—often instinctual or reflex resistance. In the end, the human brain poses a significant set of barriers that we must break through if we are to meet the increasing demands of leading change in ourselves and in others.

This is why we argue that unlocking individual change starts and ends with the mental maps people carry in their heads—how they see the organization and their world at work. Just as actual maps guide the steps people take on a hike through the Himalayas, mental maps direct people's behavior through the daily ups and downs of organizational life. And if leaders cannot change their own and others' mental maps, they will not change the destinations people pursue or the paths they take to get there. If what is in people's heads is not remapped, then their hearts and hands have nothing new to follow.

The Crux of the Challenge

This brings us to the crux of the challenge. Clearly change has always been and still remains difficult. Unless we can dig beneath the surface and get to the fundamentals of why this is so, we have no hope or prayer of meeting the ever-escalating demands for leading change.

To better understand these fundamentals of breaking through the brain barrier, we might take a page from those who broke through the sound barrier. The sound barrier was first broken in level flight on October 14, 1947, by then Captain (and today General) Chuck Yeager. Before this, several pilots died because scientists and pilots simply did not fully understand the nature of the sound barrier or, more precisely, they did not fully understand the changes in aerodynamics that occurred at transonic and supersonic speeds. Simplified, what happens is that as the plane moves faster through the air, the increased speed causes a shockwave to form on the wing and tail and change the aerodynamics of the plane. As the speed of the plane increases to nearly the speed of sound, this shockwave moves back along the wing and tail and changes the pressure distribution, and thus the plane's aerodynamic properties.

Breaking through the sound barrier required three specific adjustments to these transonic aerodynamics. First, enough thrust had to be generated to move a plane at level flight faster than the speed of sound (about 761 miles per hour at sea level). This required a change from propeller to jet propulsion. Second, to adjust for the change in aerodynamics on the wings at supersonic speed, the wings had to be swept back and made thinner. Third, to create the additional air pressure needed to cause appropriate pitch (movement of the plane's nose up or down), the horizontal stabilizers needed significant modification. The horizontal stabilizers are simply the small wings on either side of the plane's tail. Along the back edge of each is a section that swivels up or down. At subsonic flight, the movement of this small section is sufficient to cause the plane to climb or dive. This same small surface was not sufficient at transonic and supersonic speeds to generate the same affect. Today, on most supersonic planes, rather than just a small section of the trailing edge moving, the entire horizontal stabilizer pivots to create the needed air pressure change to alter the pitch during supersonic flight.

However, even with this enhanced understanding and modifications, as flights would approach the speed of sound, the plane would shake as the shock waves buffeted it. It seemed that the harder technicians and pilots pushed the planes to the sound barrier, the more resistance they encountered. Some even thought that in pushing through the sound barrier, the shock waves would crush the plane like a aluminum can.

On that eventful day in October 1947, Yeager reported that his plane was shaking violently as he approached Mach 1. However, once he "punched through it," the flight was as smooth as glass.

Take a moment to look at Figure 1.1. This incredible photo captures an F-18 fighter jet hitting Mach I, the speed of sound. Obviously, sound waves are invisible to the unaided human eye, and the only reason that we can see the plane breaking through the sound barrier is because the shock waves compress the moisture in the air to form this temporary cloud.

Figure 1.1   F18 breaking through the sound barrier.

"Interesting, but what does this have to do with leading change?" you might ask. As we interviewed and observed managers, we consistently found that there seemed to be a natural barrier to change—a brain barrier. Like the sound barrier, the faster a leader tried to push change, the more shock waves of resistance compacted together, forming a massive barrier to change. Instead of a sound barrier, though, leaders confront a "brain barrier" composed of preexisting and successful mental maps. These incredibly powerful maps determine how people see the world of work, guiding their daily steps and behaviors. Indeed, our heads are chock full of such maps, and just as the court jester shown in Figure 1.2, the maps in our head, far more than the eyes on our face, frame our personal views of the world.

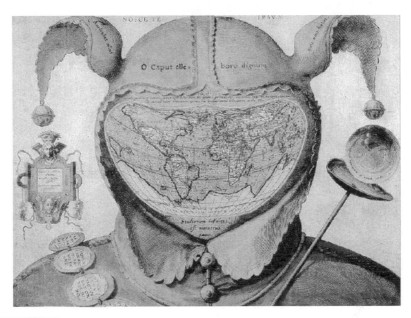

Figure 1.2 An alternative view of the world.

The power of these mental maps surprised one of our colleagues several years ago. He was hired as a consultant to help transform a meatpacking factory from an authoritarian top-down management system to a high-involvement participative one. After three days of intensive training focused on the opportunities, challenges, and everyday logistics associated with greater empowerment and self-managed work teams, a burly 300-pound butcher stood up in the back of the room, slammed a meat cleaver into the table, and demanded in no uncertain terms that he still had "a right to have a manager tell me what to do and when to do it." Clearly, this butcher's maps of his world at work had not budged an inch. And for significant organizational change to take hold of peoples' hearts and hands in this meat-packing plant—or anywhere else for that matter—leaders of change must comprehend, break through, and ultimately redraw individual mental maps, one-by-one, person-by-person, again and again.

This brings us to the critical barriers that can block sustainable strategic change. In our work, we have identified not one but three successive barriers to change. The low success rate and conversely high failure rate of change is due in part to the fact that we must break through three strong barriers for ultimate success. We refer to these three barriers as the *see*, *move*, and *finish* barriers:

- **See**. Even when opportunities or threats stare people in the face, they *fail to see* the need to change.
- **Move**. Even when they see the need, they often still *fail to move*.
- **Finish**. Even when they see the need and start to move, they often *fail to finish*—not going far or fast enough for the change to ultimately succeed.

Like the sound barrier, if we can understand the nature of each of these three barriers, we can make the needed adjustments to achieve breakthrough change. As a consequence, we build on past research as well as our interviews and work with managers to grasp why people fail to see, move, and finish. In addition, we reveal the keys to success—the modifications needed to break through each barrier. While we don't claim to have all the insights or answers, our journey has illuminated enough executives that we felt compelled to put into writing what was working in practice. Quite simply, this book reveals the forces behind each barrier to change and describes specific tools and techniques for breaking through.

Simplify and Apply

In describing these barriers and providing the tools to break through them, we try to stick to an important principle. This principle is best illustrated by Albert Einstein who said that we should make things as simple as possible, but no simpler. In our view, the eight mistakes, twelve steps, and so on about change are often right in direction, but overly complicated for reality. But wait—we just got through arguing that today's changes are bigger and more complicated than the past and that changes in the future are likely only to get more daunting. Why would simplifying change help us lead ever more complex changes? There are two convincing reasons.

First, something is practical if we can remember and recall it, especially under pressure. No matter how comprehensive a model, framework, theory, or idea, if we cannot remember and recall it under pressure in real time when application is needed, it ends up making very little practical difference. So if change is more prevalent, faster, and more unpredictable than ever before, then it is equally critical for us to take action when needed. Whatever tools we hope to use in making change succeed, we must remember, recall, and apply them in real situations, in real time, and under real pressure.

In sticking with this simplicity principle, it is important to keep in mind that long history and scientific evidence have taught us that as humans we have limitations when it comes to remembering and recalling models, frameworks, or even strings of numbers that are too long or complicated. For example, have you ever wondered why most phone numbers around the world contain only seven digits or less? It is because 80 percent of the population can remember seven digits, but that percentage drops dramatically as you add digits. In fact, while 80 percent of the world population can remember seven random digits, that quickly drops to about 2 percent by only adding three additional digits (meaning, going from to seven to ten). If a change strategy sounds great on paper but can't be remembered by people in the field, then it really isn't worth anything. For this reason, we take a very pragmatic approach in proposing a framework for leading change. We offer up a framework that can be remembered, recalled, and—most importantly—applied. Fundamentally, it has only three components.

Second, we argue for simplification because achieving 80 percent of desired results rapidly is much better than never attaining 100 percent. If 80 percent quickly is your target, then 20 percent of the factors are usually the key. For example, we commonly see cases in which 20 percent of a firm's customers account for 80 percent of its sales. In sports, we see many situations where 80 percent of the team's points come from 20 percent of its players. And while a firm cannot ignore its other customers or a team its full roster of players, both organizations get the best bang for their buck by focusing on the critical core—the fundamentals. For this reason, we focus on the most critical elements of change.

This is one of the important differentiators of this book. We keep it simple, and we focus on the fundamentals. We have found through experience in working with a variety of firms around the world that if you get the fundamentals right—the critical 20 percent—and hit 80 percent of the desired result quickly, the rest will come. Conversely, you can spend truckloads of time on all the fancy frills of change, and the ignored fundamentals will steal success away.

In the end, a complete mastery of the fundamentals is key to breakthrough change. Just as mastering the fundamentals of gravity and friction allowed designers to make the wings thinner and sweep them back on planes so pilots could break the sound barrier, mastering change fundamentals is key to breaking through the powerful and persistent mental barriers of resistance.

The Fundamentals of Change

What are the fundamental dynamics of leading strategic change? The following diagram (Figure 1.3) attempts to capture this process, and subsequent short sections describe these dynamics relative to each of the main cells in the matrix. And as we mentioned, real mastery of these concepts will come through subsequent chapters that walk you through these dynamics and explain them in much greater detail.

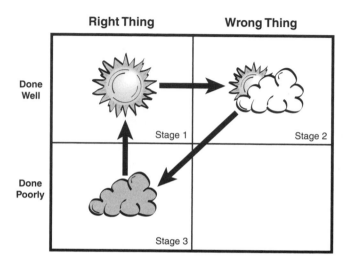

Figure 1.3 Matrix of the fundamental dynamics of change.

Virtually every major change has its roots in success (Stage 1). In almost every case, the need for change is born of past success—of doing the right thing well. The more right it is and the better it has been done, the more likely that it has a long rather than short history. For example, IBM did the right thing (making main frame computers) and did it well. It did it better than anyone else for nearly 50 years. Xerox was so closely tied to the invention and commercialization of copying that the company name became a verb ("Please xerox this document for me.").

In almost every organizational or individual case, change starts with a history of doing the right thing and doing it well. Then, often unexpectedly, something happens: the environment shifts, and the right thing becomes the wrong thing. A new competitor comes on the scene with equal quality but significantly lower price, or a new technology renders past standards of product reliability obsolete, or government regulations disallow previous business practices, or customers change their preferences, or a million and one other shifts.

As a consequence of the shift, what was once right is now wrong (an initial shift from Stage 1 to Stage 2). More importantly, and the really frustrating thing, is that while what we did right is now wrong, we are still very good at it. In IBM's case, computing power soared while cost remained constant (or dropped in real terms); and servers, minicomputers, and even desktop computers began to replace the role of some mainframes. Just making big boxes was no longer the right thing, but IBM continued doing it so well. People's hearts and souls, self-worth, and image were tied up in years and years of making "big iron" (IBM's vernacular for mainframes). This persistence to keep moving along the old successful pathways of the past constitutes the first part of change.

Then after enough pain, blood, or at least red ink on the floor, we start the second stage of change by finally recognizing that the old right thing is now the wrong thing—we finally see the light. We then begin to envision what the new right thing might be. Over time, the new right thing becomes clear. But, in almost every case, because the *new* right thing is *new*, we are usually not very good at it at first. Initially we end up doing the new right thing quite poorly. This is the third and frustrating part of change.

For example, not long after Lou Gerstner took over as CEO at IBM, people inside the company finally saw that just "selling boxes" would not work and that providing integrated solutions was critical to their future success. However, neither IBM nor its employees were good at making money from providing integrated solutions at first. While analysts today tout the importance of "solutions" in IBM's revenue and profit growth, we quickly forget that back in the early 1990s, as IBM initiated this strategic change, the *integrated solution units* (ISUs as they were called) were most closely associated with losing money, not making it.

Hopefully, after a time, we master the new right thing and start to do it well (a move from Stage 3 back to Stage 1). At this point, the sun shines again, and we bask in the warmth of its rays. Life is good. (Well, that is until life changes and the new right thing once again becomes the wrong thing.) IBM eventually did become proficient at providing integrated solutions. In fact, the service business was the largest revenue and profit growth engine for IBM during the late 1990s.

The fundamental process or cycle of change is just that simple. This is the core 20 percent that captures 80 percent of the picture:

- Stage 1: Do the right thing and do it well.
- Stage 2: Discover that the right thing is now the wrong thing.
- Stage 3: Do the new right thing, but do it poorly at first.
- Stage 4: Eventually do the new right thing well.

Anyone can understand, remember, and recall this framework. The three barriers we mentioned earlier cause the process to break down. The failure to see keeps the change process from even getting started. Even when started, the failure to move keeps us from entering the path of the new right thing. Even if we start and move, the failure to finish keeps us from doing the new right thing and doing it well.

With this overall map, the following chapters help you master the challenge of remapping change. We dive into the dynamics that drive behavior in each step of our change framework and explore the power of mental maps that can often divert us from successful change and how we can break through these brain barriers.

Specifically, in Chapter 2, "Barrier #1: Failure to See," we examine the first remapping challenge. We explore why—even when a threat or opportunity is visible—we fail to see it. Clearly, if we fail to see threats or opportunities, we will not make needed changes. In response to this challenge, in Chapter 3, "Solutions and Tools for Breaking through Barrier #1: Helping People See the Need," we detail how you can break through this barrier and help yourself and others actually see the need to change.

We explore the second remapping challenge in Chapter 4, "Barrier #2: Failure to Move." We examine why even when we see, we often fail to move. While it sounds illogical (why would someone fail to move if they saw the need?), there is ample evidence that failure to move is quite common. As a consequence, effective change must overcome this powerful mental barrier. Chapter 5, "Solutions and Tools for Breaking through Barrier #2: Helping People Make the Move," delivers the keys to overcoming this barrier and helping people actually move once they see the need to change.

The third and final remapping challenge fills Chapter 6, "Barrier #3: Failure to Finish." We explore why, even when people move, they often fail to finish—not moving far or fast enough. While recognizing the need for change is the thrust that gets us going, and moving down the new path lifts us off the ground, if the momentum cannot be maintained, the initial upward lift needed to fly is overpowered by the constant downward pull of gravity and natural resistance to change. We have seen and studied many cases in which change projects attained initial liftoff, only to falter and crash shortly after clearing the runway. Chapter 7, "Solutions and Tools for Breaking through Barrier #3: Helping People Fight through the Finish," provides a simple but effective framework for overcoming this challenge and provides specific tools that can help you break through this barrier and help people finish a major change initiative.

In Chapter 8, "Pulling It All Together," we combine and integrate all the specific components that we discuss separately up to that point to ensure that you can apply these fundamental principles of change in real situations, which don't come so neatly divided as chapters in a book. In most of these examples in Chapter 8, we examine how using the principles can help you remap your organization for greater revenue and profit growth.

Chapter 9, "Getting Ahead of the Change Curve," provides the glue to ensure that all this sticks—sticks together and sticks to you, the reader. This glue is essentially a tool that you can use to gauge where you and others are in the change process and what might need to be done to ensure the targeted change succeeds. The tool is not only something you can use to lead change, but is also something you can use to train, educate, and empower others to meet this challenge as well.

2

Barrier #1: Failure to See

Just imagine. You are relaxing on the beach; the sun is shining; its rays shimmering off the ocean waves as they lazily breaking on the shore. A cooling breeze occasionally rustles the palm trees. You are in this idyllic spot because you've done it the old-fashioned way—you've earned it. You've worked hard; you've been smart. Your company is touted in the press as one of the most admired. You are the market leader in what is expected to be one of the largest consumer market products ever—the cell phone. At its unveiling, your StarTac phone instantly becomes *the* phone to own. You are Motorola.

You are doing the right thing and doing it well. This was the case for Motorola into the early nineties. Its analog phones were the phones to own, and Motorola dominated the industry with a global market share of more than 30 percent at its peak.

But then the environment shifted—radically. First, a new digital technology for mobile phones came along. However, early on it was not clear how superior it would be. In addition, the new digital technology would require literally billions of dollars of infrastructure investment. Most U.S. carriers, such as Sprint and Verizon, did not seem to want to make this investment, and it would make little sense to produce a phone that would not work on the carriers' systems. Perhaps this is why none of the other U.S. mobile phone makers leaped in this new digital direction at first. Although European carriers did seem as though they would embrace the new technology, any individual country such as Germany or France paled in comparison to the market size of the United States, so why worry about what the Europeans might do?

The second shift involved the emergence of a new competitor. Although the new competitor was pushing the new technology, to many this seemed more an act of desperation than foresight. The company had just been through a serious internal leadership shake-up, including the suicide of its CEO in 1990. The new CEO installed in 1992, Jorma Olilla, was a former banker and certainly not a technologist. So what if he was making some noise about focusing on mobile communication, which represented less than 2 percent of Nokia's total revenue at the time. The vast majority of its revenue came from forest products, and it had been that way for more than 100 years. The company also excelled at making rubber boots for fishermen. So what in the world could it know about high tech? To top it off, the new competitor was based somewhere in frozen Finland, a country with a total population less than the city of Chicago. Besides, no one was really sure how to pronounce the company's name—Nokia. Was it Nó-kia (with the emphasis on the "No") or No-kiá (with the emphasis on the "kia")?

The result? Motorola's first reaction was to flat-out deny that this new competitor or technology was anything to worry about.

But then Nokia's revenue increased four-fold from $2.1 billion in 1993 to $8.7 billion in 1997. All of Europe adopted a common digital standard that allowed people to use mobile phones virtually anywhere in the region. This convenience drove even greater demand. In the meantime, the fragmented U.S. standards meant that one phone would not necessarily work in every state, which caused a dampening effect on growth. Nokia also decided to emphasize brand and brand management as much as technology. It focused on seemingly innocent items like making the user interface intuitive (such as a green key for "send" and red for "end call") and consistent across all its models. In 1998, just six years after it decided to push into the global mobile phone market, Nokia moved from not even being in the race to taking over the number 1 position and passed Motorola in terms of units sold globally.

What did Motorola do? Oddly, it put even more investment and effort into analog phones. It did what it knew how to do—what it was good at doing—and it did it even more intensely than before.

Well, we all know what happened after that. In just six short years (between 1998 and 2003), Motorola's global share of mobile phones plummeted by more than *50 percent*! During this same period, Nokia, virtually unknown in the U.S. in the early nineties (or most of the rest of the world for that matter) gathered steam to become one of the top ten recognized brands in the world behind the likes of Coca-Cola and McDonald's. In 2001, with a market share of around 35 percent, Nokia's profit share (i.e., share of all money made in the industry) was nearly 70 percent. So while one in every three phones sold were Nokia phones, seven in every ten dollars (euro, yen, markka, etc.) in profits went to Nokia. That's right: Nokia's "profit share" doubled their "market share."

If only the story ended here, but, it doesn't. While Nokia was busy taking over the world and dethroning Motorola, a company that wasn't even making mobile phones when Nokia's CEO, Jorma Olilla, took over in 1992, quietly began to move in 1998 just as Nokia was overtaking Motorola with nearly 40 million total units sold to Motorola's nearly 35 million. The company was Samsung, and in 1998 it held a mere 2.7 percent of the global world market and sold just 4.7 million phones. However, even this number failed to capture Nokia's attention because Samsung sold most of its phones at home in Korea. As a consequence, no one, and certainly not Nokia in 1998, predicted Samsung would rise to challenge Motorola for the number two spot in the world among mobile phone makers by 2006.

No one saw Samsung coming, including Nokia, until it was a bit too late. Samsung's real surge started in 2002. While other manufacturers dismissed a new capability of putting small but low-quality cameras in phones, Samsung put into action the old saying: "A picture is worth a thousand words." Samsung executives grasped that people did not want phones to replace cameras but simply wanted an additional, more information-rich means of mobile communication with friends and family. And so in six startling years, Samsung raced from selling a mere 21 million phones in 2000 to 104 million in 2005, and its global market share nearly tripled from 5 to 13 percent!

In every case, shareholders paid a dear price for the failure to see the need to change. As Motorola was blindsided by the surge of Nokia, Motorola shareholders saw their value drop by 50 percent between

1997 and the end of 2002. During the same period, Nokia shareholders watched their value increase by 300 percent. Likewise, as Nokia was stunned by the explosion of Samsung onto the world mobile phone stage, between 2002 and the end of 2005, Nokia shareholders gasped as the value of their stock drop by 26 percent. During this same period, Samsung shareholders grinned as they saw the value of their shares soar by 216 percent.

How this three-way battle will shake out is anyone's guess. In 2006, both Nokia and a revitalized Motorola pushed ahead and placed a bit more distance between themselves and Samsung. However, it will be interesting to see how well they've learned their lessons or whether all three will be blindsided by Apple, which announced its new iPhone on January 9, 2007. We make no predictions, but odds are that past success will cause someone to miss something critical relative to needed changes to sustain success in the future.

Blinded by the Light

It is no brilliant statement to say that if you do not see the need to change, you will not change. Everyone knows this. But if everyone knows this, why do so many change initiatives fail to break through this first barrier? Stated simply, we fail at breaking through this first barrier of change *not* because we don't know it is there but because *we underestimate its strength*. We underestimate its strength because we fail to take the time or effort to understand fully its nature.

So why don't we see the truck racing toward us, or the treasure of gold beneath our feet? Why could Motorola not see the threat of Nokia? Why did Nokia miss the rise of Samsung? Were these just invisible events? Were they simply impossible for anyone to see? These might seem like silly questions, but if a particular demand for change were invisible, then we could hardly blame ourselves or someone else for not seeing it. But in most cases, the need for change is visible—if only we would see it. Again, why do we fail to see the need for change? Fundamentally, *we fail to see because we are blinded by the light of what we already see.*

To explain, let's return to Motorola. (By the way, we do not mean to pick on Motorola. They do not stand alone by any means in missing a significant threat or opportunity. At different points in time, firms such as AT&T, Black & Decker, Caterpillar, IBM, Kmart, Lucent, Merrill

Lynch, Sony, Xerox, and others have not seen the need to change as early as they might have and have paid the price—as have their shareholders.) Still, while Motorola is not the only firm to miss an important threat or opportunity, the threats and opportunities Motorola faced were hardly invisible. Yet Motorola still did not see, recognize, or acknowledge them until after the cost of waiting was significant. Instead, Motorola first denied the threat and then worked harder at what it knew how to do well (see Figure 2.1).

So why do we deny? When we see evidence that a strategy, structure, technology, or product was right in the past but now is wrong, why do we ignore and deny the evidence?

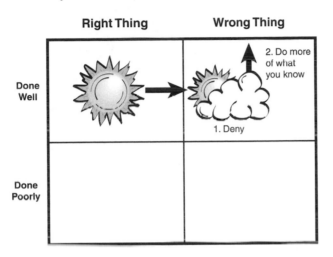

Figure 2.1 Key tendencies when the right thing becomes the wrong thing.

Remember, we fail to see the need for change because we are blinded by the light of what we already see. Virtually every major personal or company change rarely occurs in isolation but contains a context, a history. In virtually every case, individuals or companies were doing the right thing and doing it well before something in the environment changed. Just as the previous right thing did not come from out of the blue, neither did our ability to do it well. Our ability to do the old right thing well developed over time. Likewise, the maps we used to guide our actions were developed and reinforced by success over time. With success these mental maps came to guide our behaviors as concretely as physical maps guide the steps we take on a wilderness trek. Our mental maps tell U.S. where to go and how to get there. For example, consider the map in Figure 2.2.

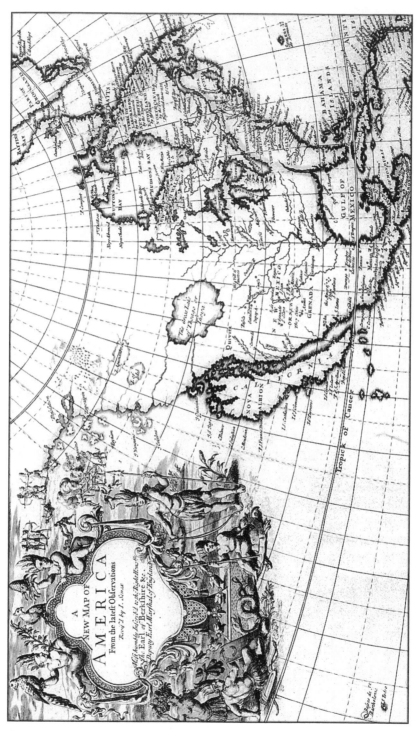

Figure 2.2 Map of the Island of California.

This is a map of the island of California. Many people, when they first see it, think it is a futuristic map of California after a huge earthquake—what Californians refer to as the "great quake to come." The map is actually quite old.

For centuries, Europeans were captivated by legends of distant islands with unimaginable wealth. In 1541, Hernán Cortés and a group of adventurers set sail from Spain to discover such an island. Cortés sailed across the Atlantic, portaged through Mexico, and then set sail again up the Strait of California, more commonly known today as the Gulf of Baja. Eventually, his provisions ran low, his crew grew nervous, and he was forced to turn back. To better understand this, it may be helpful to remember that the Gulf of Baja (also called the Sea of Cortez) is nearly 1,000 miles or more than 1600 kilometers long, and the sailing is slow because the winds between two mainlands, modern-day Mexico and the Baja peninsula, stay weak and inconsistent.

For Cortés, failure was unacceptable, and so with a little wishful thinking he created a success. To the east was land and to the west was land; to the north and south, water. Cortés reached a perfectly logical conclusion: he was in search of an island, and an island he had found—La Isla de California. Cortés returned to Spain and reported to the king and queen exactly what they wanted to hear (and what he wanted to believe): *California is an island.*

Shortly after Cortés's discovery, another expedition was launched to confirm his claim. This one traveled far up along the Pacific coast, past present-day San Francisco. This overly ambitious expedition also ran low on supplies, and by the time they reached the Mendocino River on northern California's coast, the crew was stricken with scurvy. With no inclination to dispute Cortés and no absolute evidence that he was wrong, they concluded that the Mendocino River was really a strait separating the northern part of the island of California from the rest of the continent.

Just imagine if you had this map and landed in what is present-day eastern Texas along the Gulf of Mexico. Your objective is to travel overland and reach the island of California. What would you need to take with you? Boats, of course. You would have to haul boats more than 2,500 kilometers (more than 1,500 miles) across what are present-day Texas, New Mexico, and the deserts of Arizona, only to discover that California was not an island. In fact, several expeditions after

Cortés provided clear proof that California was not an island. Still, how long did this map of the Island of California persist? One hundred years? One hundred and fifty years? No, this cartographic myth persisted throughout Europe for more than two centuries, until in 1745 a royal proclamation from Spain finally declared: "California is *not* an island." (Keep in mind this was just a few years before the American colonies declared independence.)

Why did it take so long for this map to change? Once the belief that California was an island had been established, reports from later explorers were filtered to fit the existing map; anything contradictory was labeled false or impossible. For all the king knew, the map worked quite well. Why should he throw it away? Similarly, for Motorola, analog phones had worked quite well for a long time. Black, clam-shell phones with little thought about consistent brand characteristics or easy user interface provided a successful map for more than a decade. Why should Motorola throw away this great map?

Again, this phenomenon is not restricted to companies, nor is it a disease that only infects senior executives. It can and does happen in all sizes of firms and at all levels of positions. To appreciate this we only have to think of some individual examples.

Consider the transition from individual contributor to manager of individual contributors. Managers consistently tell us it is one of the most difficult. Why? Simplified, as an individual contributor you get things done by doing them yourself. If you are a salesperson, you get the sale by going out and making the pitch and closing the deal yourself. Over time, you establish a personalized set of maps for navigating this individual contributor territory. However, as a sales team manager, you must transition from doing things yourself to getting them done through others; you must change from motivating yourself to motivating others. Because the situation has changed (you've been promoted), what was clearly the right thing before (i.e., doing things yourself) has become the wrong thing, but you are still very good at doing it!

Or consider someone who was very successful at conveying subtle hints and cues in his communication and thereby never risking open embarrassment to anyone in public with whom he might disagree. This individual was known as a master communicator in his native Japan. He had years of success in Tokyo and developed an intricate, first-rate map for guiding his communication effectively. His map also led him to determine that those who demonstrated less tact and sophistication were untrustworthy with sensitive issues or assignments. This individual was subsequently transferred to an attractive new position a few kilometers to the south—Melbourne. Sadly, his carefully constructed, well tested communication map did not work so well in Australia. While he worked hard at communicating with great sensitivity and subtlety, "locals" perceived him as not being direct and therefore untrustworthy. In turn, while the locals "said what they meant and meaning what they said," as they thought they should do, he viewed them as insensitive to others' feelings and a bit immature and self-centered in their communication. Not surprisingly, the assignment did not go well. Yet, this individual manager was slow to see that what was once very right was now very wrong. He was slow to see that a serious personal change was needed if he were to continue to succeed in this new and different environment.

Thus, the first and critical point about why we fail to see the need for change stems from the fact that we stand blinded by the light of successful past mental maps. The longer these maps have worked, the more it makes sense to hold on to them and the more difficult it is to see beyond them to recognize the need for changing them. This applies not only to companies and macro issues like strategies or technology, but also to individuals and issues as small as how to communicate or provide feedback to someone.

Placing Ourselves at the Center

The first brain barrier of failing to see the need for change is amplified by the fact that not only do we hold on to past maps but we also tend to put our maps in the center of the universe with everything else revolving around them. To illustrate the point personally, take a moment to draw a map of the world. It doesn't need to be an elaborate one; just quickly sketch out the continents of the world. Now, and only if you're done, take a careful look at your map. In fact, draw a line down the center of the map. Where is the line placed? Is it running through the Atlantic Ocean? Pacific? Is it crossing the Americas or India? Europe or Asia? When we do this simply exercise with executives around the world, you might guess the results. Asian executives put themselves in the center of the map, Americans do the same, and Europeans follow suit. Whether we like it or not, we mostly live by mental maps that make where we live the center of the universe. This is not only true for mental maps but for physical ones as well.

If you want to do something fun the next time you are in a foreign country, wander into a map store and take a look at a world map produced by publishers in that country. Invariably, the map will place that particular country in the center of the world. This tendency has a long tradition. Perhaps it is best illustrated with an old map of the Central or Middle Kingdom—China. The two Chinese characters that constitute the name "China" literally mean "central" or "middle kingdom." As the map in Figure 2.3 illustrates, China saw herself at the center of the world then as well as now.

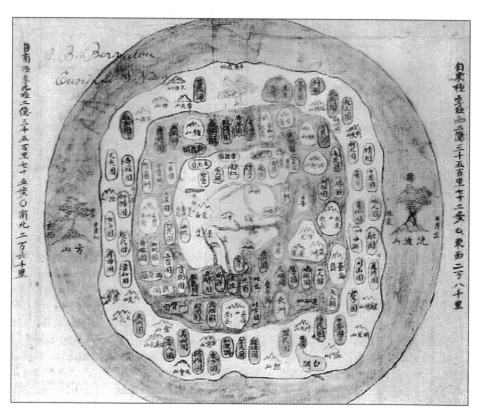

Figure 2.3 Chinese view of the world.

Now consider a modern illustration of this mapping phenomenon in the case of IKEA. IKEA's mission is to create a better everyday life for as many people as possible by making beautiful, functional items for consumers' homes at the lowest possible price. It launched its first catalog in Sweden in 1951. Since then, it has expanded into 22 countries across Europe, North America, Southeast Asia, and Australia. In 2005, it had sales of nearly $18 billion. In sync with its philosophy and mission, its competitive strategy is based on a value proposition of moderate to good quality Scandinavian-design furniture at incredibly low prices. Standardization in process and manufacturing helps keep costs low, which in turn drives the company's ability to offer consumers a low price. This strategy works well around the world for most of the products that IKEA offers, such as curtains or dinnerware. However, when expanding into the United States, IKEA failed miserably on a few items, specifically beds and sheets.

When IKEA began its U.S. operations, it shipped low-priced, moderate-quality, *metric*-sized beds and bedding to all U.S. stores. It advertised how wonderful the beds were—especially at a full 2 meters in length! IKEA expected the same great success in the U.S. that they had enjoyed in Europe. Unfortunately, sales did not go well at first. What was IKEA's response? Increase its advertising.

How did beds and bedding then sell in the U.S.? They quickly became category failures, filling up entire warehouses. Local store and regional managers tried to communicate to corporate headquarters in Sweden that metric-sized beds and bedding would not sell in the United States—in spite of the fact that they were priced lower than the king, queen, full, and twin-size bedding found in competitors' furniture stores.

How did IKEA's senior managers, who were seven time zones away at corporate headquarters, respond to this local dilemma? "Be more creative. *Pull* the customers into your store. Any good retailer *can* sell metric-sized bedding; that's the solution to your inventory problems." Anders Dahlvig, CEO of IKEA, is quoted as saying, "Whether we are in China, Russia, Manhattan, or London, people buy the same things. We don't adapt to local markets."[1] So despite local and regional U.S. managers' constant attempts to convince headquarters otherwise, their bosses in Sweden clung to their tried-and-true map. How long did this map that metric was king and the center of the universe persist? One

[1] Nicholas George, "One furniture store fits all." *Financial Times*, February 8, 2001, p. 11.

month? Six months? Twelve months? No. This mental map persisted for more than two years. Finally, with bursting warehouses, the metric-sized beds and bedding were reluctantly discontinued in the U.S. market, and management declared that metric was *not* king; king was king; queen was king; twin was king in the U.S. market.

Why did IKEA persist in following its map of metric as king? Because it had worked so well in the past. They were good at it; they placed it in the center of their universe and viewed everything else revolving around it. Company leaders could not see an alternative map because their vision was full of the successful working map they already had.

An important thing to appreciate is that when placing ourselves at the center of the map, we almost always distort what revolves around it. "We" become disproportionately large, and other things shrink and twist in relation. This can in turn lead U.S. to focus on and exaggerate what fits our view of the world and discount or even ignore what fails to fit onto our world map.

We might think of IKEA as having also viewed the world this way. As its CEO pointed out, "We don't adapt to local markets." While IKEA clearly realized the size and opportunity of the U.S. market, IKEA persisted in seeing itself and its metric measurements as the center of the world. Everything else revolved around it.

As already stated, you only get a centered map established and accepted if it works. Metric measures had worked well for more than 30 years. In fact, IKEA's metric approach worked as well in the U.S. for most of the other items the company carried as it had for the past three decades in Europe. For example, IKEA effectively sold metric chairs all around the world, including in the U.S.. No one in the U.S. cared (or even knew) that most chairs IKEA sold were .78 meters from the floor to the seat. The more this metric map works, the more you begin to believe that the world revolves around you. With metrics at the center of the universe and with literally billions of dollars of success behind it, why would executives at IKEA *not* resist changing the map? Of course they would resist, and they did.

We need to be careful, however, in providing so many large company examples that we create the impression that only big organizations are subject to these mistakes. We also see individuals operate with central position maps all the time. For example, we knew of a manager sent on an international assignment who had "speak up" at the center of his mental map of interpersonal effectiveness. He explained that "speak up" was the phrase he used (and that the company used) to describe in shorthand the belief that the best way to make decisions, resolve conflicts, and communicate in general was to speak up, to say what you mean and mean what you say. This, he explained, included silence. If you weren't saying anything, then it meant that you had nothing to say.

This manager from Alberta, Canada, was then sent to Thailand. Unfortunately, most Thai workers did not share his same mental map of effective interpersonal relations. They were often silent when they, in fact, had things to say. Specifically, they were often silent when they disagreed with this individual. They even said *yes* (they agreed) when they really meant *no* they did not. It did not take this manager long to discover that people said nothing when they in fact did have something to say because their later actions did not follow what he thought their silence had meant. As these types of experiences began to pile up, he concluded that "Thais do not say what they mean and I can't trust them to mean what they say. I'm afraid that many are just dishonest, weak, and two-faced. With employees like this, I'm not sure we can ever succeed in this country." He was right. The company had difficulty being successful. However, the firm's struggles were not due to Thai employees, but rather its country manager.

His mistaken interpretation was to a large extent driven by putting his map at the center of the universe and making everything else revolve around it, and in the process what revolved around his center became distorted and misinterpreted. Given his interpretation of Thai employees, his course of action was to send some key employees to a training program on speaking up. He pushed what he knew and pushed it hard. Interestingly, the more the employees learned about speak up from the training program, the more they resisted it because they did not think it would work with their Thai subordinates, and they did not want to try it and fail. At the center of their map was Bangkok, not Calgary.

Speak up for this country manager in Thailand, like metric for IKEA, was at the center of his universal map. Things in the past had successfully revolved around this center. The common elements in these situations are that when the map begins to fail, whether it's Motorola, IKEA, or an individual manager, the common first reaction is to deny the failure and then try harder by doing even more of what you know how to do best.

Distorting Our View

As noted, by "centering" our maps we distort what we force to revolve around it. In general, distorted maps have a tendency to exaggerate some elements of the terrain while diminishing others. This typically reflects the psychological process—found even in cartography—of inflating what you know and deflating what you do not. From a mental map perspective, the extreme state is one in which you believe that what you know is everything, and what you do not know is nothing.

How do distorted maps actually look in the world of cartography? Consider the map of the United States in Figure 2.4 from a Bostonian's view.

Figure 2.4 Bostonian's view of the United States.

As you can see, Cape Cod holds significant size and substance in their mind. On the other hand, while Florida exists, it's quite small in comparison. Likewise, the Northeast in particular and the East in general are much larger than the humble (though at least it is not an island anymore) California.

Just in case we have any Bostonian readers who are not quite sure what is wrong with this picture, we have also added a map that more accurately portrays the relative dimensions and size of the places in question (see Figure 2.5).

Figure 2.5 A more accurate view of the United States.

This tendency is not confined to Bostonians; we all quite commonly distort physical and mental maps this way. Asked to draw a map of their neighborhood, people invariably draw their street and house much larger than they actually are in proportion to the overall neighborhood that they map out.

While this type of mistaken map is intriguing, the key question is how does it apply to the business world? The first important implication is that while a distorted map may be mistaken, it still works as long as one does not venture outside of the known area. The distorted map of the U.S. in Figure 2.4 is not a problem and works well—as long as you stay in New England. Venture off to Florida and use this map to calculate driving time, and you run into trouble. It takes much longer to drive the length of Florida than the Bostonian's distorted map would lead you to believe.

The second important implication is that the distorted map leads you to stay within the exaggerated area. Why would you want to leave Boston or New England? After all, based on the map, it looks as though there really is not much else out there. Consequently, using this mistaken map would quite likely cause you to stay at home. Ironically, staying at home increases the map's distorted success. The more you use the map to get around at home, the more successful experiences you would have, and the more convinced you become that you should hang on to this map no matter where you venture. Following the distorted map actually keeps you from encountering evidence of the map's inaccuracies and mistakes.

It is relatively easy to find business examples of companies relying on mistaken, distorted maps. An interesting example is the Kellogg Company. Located in Battlecreek, Michigan, Kellogg has dominated the breakfast table of Americans (especially children) for decades. Kellogg owned a mental map of the world that exaggerated what it knew (breakfast cereal in the U.S.) and deflated what it did not know (other food products for the rest of the world). As a consequence, the world of Kellogg's existing and new products as well as existing and new markets looked like what you see in Figure 2.6.

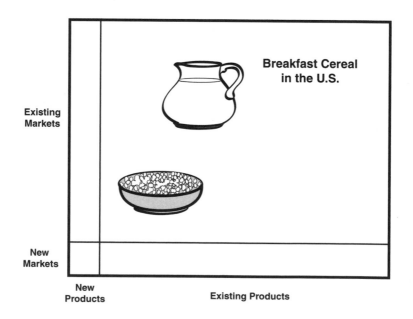

Figure 2.6 Kellogg's map of the world.

Just as a Bostonian exaggerated the size of Cape Cod, Kellogg greatly inflated the size of breakfast cereal in the U.S. compared to the rest of the picture. For nearly 40 years this map worked well at Kellogg. As a matter of fact, given how small the rest of the world and other products besides cereal seemed based on this map, why on earth should Kellogg venture far from "home," either in terms of products or markets? The prize outside "home" looked way too small to worry about. So, they didn't; they stayed at home within the safe boundaries of their seemingly successful map.

What happens, though, when the home market starts to shift? What happens when people eat breakfast less at the table and more on the run? What happens if generic makers of cereal increase their quality until they begin to rival Kellogg's and offer prices 20–30 percent below Kellogg's? What do you do if you're an executive at Kellogg? Based on the pattern we've described, at first you deny! You tell yourself, "This is just a temporary blip." If it ends up being more than temporary, you convince yourself that it is confined to a small segment of the market and it's nothing to lose sleep over.

What do you do when you see sales start to flag then flatten and you simply cannot deny the shifts in the environment? You do what you know how to do, of course. You increase trade promotions (money for retailers to push your product) to drive more cold cereal sales. This is exactly what Kellogg did, but unfortunately it did not increase sales much, and actually hurt company earnings.

Based on Kellogg's distorted mental map of the world, would you explore new products? Look at how small that space is. The answer is that you wouldn't, and Kellogg didn't. The company did not introduce a single new brand between 1983 and 1991. Even though it successfully introduced Pop-Tarts in 1964, it did not create a single new snack-food success until more than a quarter of a century later when it launched NutriGrain cereal bars in 1992.

What about new markets? Based on Kellogg's distorted mental map, would you aggressively explore new markets? Again, look at how small that space is. In talking with executives at Kellogg, several pointed out that they were "into" international markets in a big way during the eighties and nineties. The company was operating in roughly 30 different countries. But if you measured revenues and profits and not just countries in which Kellogg operated, the strategic, financial, and marketing emphases were all completely in harmony with the distorted mental map; the vast majority of efforts and returns were focused on the *home* market.

From this case example of Kellogg, let's review several key points:

- First, just because a map works does not mean that it accurately reflects all the terrain. Breakfast cereal in the U.S. was not nearly as large as it seemed to Kellogg's executives in the context of the overall breakfast-food territory.

- Second, as long as the terrain in focus doesn't change and you don't venture outside the exaggerated area of focus, the map (mistaken as it may be) continues to work fairly well. The longer it works, the more convinced you become that it is indeed correct and not distorted.

- Third, even when signs start to emerge that the map is not working as well today as it did in the past, its distorted nature creates a logical incentive to stay at home. After all, if the non-cereal and non-U.S. parts of the map are as small as they appear, then they are not really worth venturing into.

- Fourth, even as evidence starts to mount that the terrain has shifted and the map is plain wrong, there are great pressures to respond to shifts by doing exactly what you already know how to do—rather than venturing into unknown territories or paths. Just as Kellogg flooded the market with sales promotions rather than make serious attempts to launch new products or conquer new lands, *we go with what we know.*

Until Kellogg changed its mental mapmaker (new CEO Carlos Gutierrez), it saw no threat or opportunity because Kellogg was so blinded by the light of what it already saw. Later in the book, we will continue the Kellogg story and show how it eventually changed its corporate map and made breakthrough changes to transform the fortunes of the company and its shareholders.

Upright Maps

Whether a mental map is correct or mistaken, the longer it works, the harder it is to change. In a sense, all mental maps successful enough to be retained take on a final characteristic that we see in the world of cartography as well as business. This is the tendency to believe that the only way to *see* the map is the way it *has been* seen. This is important enough to bear repeating: We mistakenly think that *the only way to see a map in the future is the way it has been seen in the past.* For example, consider the map in Figure 2.7. Most people when they first see the map in Figure 2.7 instantly think that it is upside down. After all, Australia is not "up over," it is "down under."

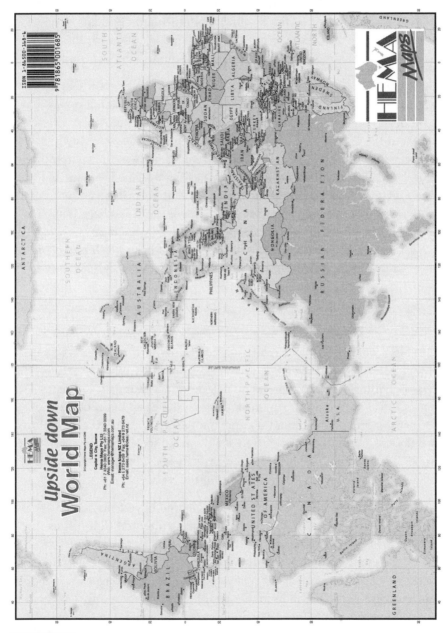

Figure 2.7 An Australian view of the world.

But consider for a moment if you were an alien traveling from a far off galaxy and stopped your spacecraft by the moon to look at our world. Would north necessarily be up? In zero gravity, isn't it just as reasonable for Australia to be up over as down under? The logical answer is of course, "Yes." However, when we show this map to people around the world, we invariably find them tilting their heads to one side until the world starts to look right side up again—with the exception of Australians who think it looks quite right just the way it is.

Still, the important thing to keep in mind is that if we see a map a certain way often enough, we end up believing that it is not *a map* but *THE map*. The longer we see the world as consisting mostly of breakfast cereal in the U.S., the easier it is to believe that is the *only* way to see the world. The longer we see metric measured beds as the center of the world, the easier it is to see metric beds as the *only* beds for the world. The longer we see "saying what you mean and meaning what you say" as the path to effective communication, the easier it is to see it as the *only* path for effective communication wherever you are in the world. Given enough time and exposure to any map, it becomes the one and only "right" map. As a result, we drastically diminish our capacity to see the world any other way.

Summary

Our main points in this chapter are straightforward. First, to break through the sound barrier, we must understand the power of shock waves that invisibly seem to hold back the plane from exceeding the speed of sound. Likewise, to break through the first "brain barrier" of change, we must understand that people will not change if they fail to see the need and they often fail to see the need for change because they are blinded by the light of what they already see—the powerful mental maps that have worked well for them in the past.

Second, we pointed out that even when people have constructed successful mental maps, those maps are quite often flawed. Just as in actual cartography, people typically put themselves at the center of their maps and in the process often distort the view by exaggerating what they know and deflating what they do not. The longer these maps have been at work, the more likely people see them not only as a map but as the only map. Unless we understand the general nature and power of mental maps, we will continue to fail to break through barrier #1, not because we don't know it is there but because we underestimate its strength.

And here we should be clear that when we say "we," we mean all of us. The phenomenon is not confined to lumbering, bureaucratic multinational dinosaurs, nor is it restricted to oxygen-deprived top executives sitting up there in the rarified thin air on companies' top floors. While it might seem comforting to think that "failing to see" is a problem for others and not ourselves, sadly, just as comfort food delivers only a fleeting effect but provides no lasting nourishment, so too do comfort thoughts leave U.S. empty in the end. What happened to Motorola or Encyclopedia Britannica or to the person in Melbourne or the other one in Thailand can happen to any one of us. We are all potentially vulnerable because the force behind failure to see threats or opportunities has nothing to do with being big or important and has everything to do with simply being human.

3

three

Solutions and Tools for Breaking through Barrier #1: Helping People See the Need

If people are blinded, how can you help them see the need to change? How can you break through the barrier of past mental maps? The solution comes in two parts—contrast and confrontation.

Both stem from basic knowledge about how we see physical objects. To see physical objects, we need some contrast in shape, light, and color. Take away differences in color or shape, or turn off the lights, and what can you see? Not much. The objects might still be there, but without contrast we can't see them. Additionally, we also see best those objects that are directly in front of us rather than off to the side (in our peripheral vision). Even though in the context of individual and organizational change we are not talking about seeing physical objects, the same two factors that help us see physical things also help us surface mental maps and see new business realities just as powerfully.

Contrast

Contrast is a key means by which the human eye distinguishes different objects. Combined differences in shape, brightness, and color give us contrast. The letters on this page stand out because of the contrast between black and white. It is such a simple notion that we generally take it for granted. But notice how the contrast lessens as you look at the circles from left to right in Figure 3.1.

Figure 3.1 Effects of contrast.

In this simple example, the different levels of contrast are easy to see. In complex organizational settings, however, there are so many things to look at that people can selectively focus on easily seen elements from the past and present that are similar (and familiar) rather than different. In effect, they can choose to ignore key contrasts and thereby avoid looking at why what worked so well in the past might fail in the future. This brings us to the second clue for overcoming the failure to see—*confrontation.*

Confrontation

Precisely because the organizational and business realities we face are complex, people can ignore or literally be blind to the "obvious" differences between their mental maps of the past and future. This is why others (and even ourselves) fail to see the reasons that strategies, structures, cultural values, processes, technologies, personal leadership styles, communication approaches, etc. should change. Further, the fact that most people do not easily see such contrasts is clear and compelling evidence that people cannot be left on their own to visualize them. Just as we "forced" you to see the contrasts among circles on the previous page, leaders must *confront* their people and sometimes themselves with key contrasts between the past, present, and future versions of the world.

The essence of confrontation is as simple as it is powerful. Just as people see most clearly what is directly in front of them, people see mentally what they most directly experience. Why? The most vivid and deep images in our minds are put there by a combination of direct physical senses. Simply, the more senses involved (seeing, hearing, touching, tasting, smelling), the deeper the impression or literal image in our minds. Thus, in this way we use the term "confrontation" not in the sense of a quarrel, but in the sense of an inescapable experiential encounter laden with new input. Simplistically, you can think of the degree of confrontation going up proportionately with the degree of physical senses involved in experiencing the contrast.

Combining Contrast and Confrontation

Figure 3.2 helps illustrate why both contrast and confrontation are necessary to overcome the first gravitational force—the failure to see.

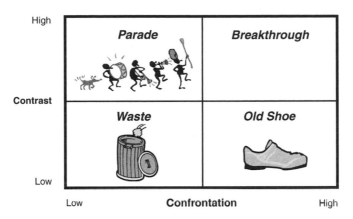

Figure 3.2 The combination of contrast and confrontation.

If people experience low contrast and low confrontation, then change efforts will likely be a waste of time, money, and energy. If what is different today versus tomorrow is not clear and there is just some email about it, this low level of contrast and confrontation will *not* cause people to see a need for change; and, consequently, they won't change.

If contrast is high, however, and confrontation is low, it is like a passing parade. People will "ooh" and "ahh" at the difference for a moment, but when the parade passes, they will go right back to what they were doing before. You have no doubt seen a new strategy or structure "parade" that captured people's attention for a minute or two, but because they did not literally experience the contrast and simply read an email or heard a presentation about it, the parade failed to engage them and ultimately failed to break through the first barrier of change.

On the other hand, if confrontation is high but contrast low, it is like an old smelly shoe. It smells and looks obviously worn out, so you notice it, but it is still the same old, comfortable shoe that has been there day after day after day, so what's new? What's different? Why should anything change? The low contrast coupled with high confrontation rarely succeeds in breaking through and helping people see the need for change.

The key to overcoming the failure to see is creating both high contrast *and* high confrontation. Unfortunately, this is much easier said than done in part because managers commit two common mistakes.

Mistake #1: The Comprehensiveness Mistake

In creating high contrast, one of the first mistakes many leaders make is what we call the *Comprehensiveness Mistake*. The mistake happens as leaders try to illustrate the contrasts between yesterday and tomorrow, but end up making the illustration too complex and comprehensive. When presented with a complex picture of the past and present (or future), the complexity actually allows employees to focus easily on some elements of the complex picture and ignore others. Because people are programmed to hang on to what has worked, they are likely to use that discretion to focus on similarities in the picture rather than differences. Why? Similarities reinforce past mental maps, while differences may threaten them. Presenting too complex a picture allows people to selectively see what they want to and then conclude, "Things are not really that different. I don't really need to change." The important thing to keep in mind is that the more complex the picture is, the more alternative specific points there are on which people can choose to focus. This, in turn, increases the chances that they will select the wrong elements in the map for guiding their actions.

What causes leaders to make this common Comprehensiveness Mistake? In some cases, the cause comes from leaders knowing that reality is complex and not wanting to appear simple-minded. Consequently, they list and discuss "a variety of factors contributing to our need to change." At one level this is quite understandable and sensible. Yet, in our experience the true cause of this mistake is less admirable. In most cases, the mistake has *less* to do with a desire to "reflect the complex reality" and *more* to do with leaders' inability or unwillingness to determine with some rigor the critical core of the issue. Rather than take the time and energy to identify the core 20 percent that accounts for 80 percent of the problems, they slip into an easier approach of simply listing all the factors. The time and brainpower required to create a long list of factors falls far short of that required to determine which factors on that long list exert the most influence. This is why calling this the Comprehensiveness Mistake is too polite; we probably ought to call it the "Laundry List Mistake."

Mistake #2: The "I Get It" Mistake

Even if we, as leaders, are successful at avoiding the first mistake (the Comprehensiveness Mistake), there is a second pitfall we all too often fall into—the "I Get It" Mistake. This mistake is simple: It is the mistake of thinking that because "you get it" others will as well.

When we say "you," we mean all of us. No one seems totally immune from making this mistake. So why do we make this mistake? The answer lies in giving ourselves too much credit. What do we mean by this? The reality is that even though we may see something and "get it" for now, we didn't see it or get it earlier. In fact, rarely do we see or instantly get something the first time we look at it. Put differently, after we spend time trying to understand a problem and the light bulb in our head finally turns on, we give ourselves too much credit and forget how much time and effort we took to "get it." This happens in part because once we get it, we get it. Once the neural connections among the various components of the problem and solution are tied together in our brain, they connect. Once we have hacked through the ambiguous brush, the path is cleared. With a bit more internal reflection, the neural dirt path becomes paved. Once the neural pathways are paved, we can travel the expressway that links the points together at autobahn speeds. The picture is now clear; we see it instantaneously. In fact, we often think, "This was so obvious. Why didn't I see it from the start?" It is as though once the light goes on, it turns off our memory of how we got there and how much time and effort it took. We forget that while we were hacking our way through the brush and trees trying to see the need for change and what the change needed to be, there were moments when we had absolutely no idea where we were going.

Consequently, we think that if we mention the need for change once to someone, they will get it, too. The need for the new vision, strategy, structure, technology, or whatever is so obvious, how many times should we have to repeat it? During consulting engagements, we have heard leaders on many occasions ask us something similar to the following: "Didn't they hear me? I explained all this in my presentation the other day. Are they brain-dead?" The answer, of course, is, "No, they are not." The problem is that to fully engage the brain you need to send a consistent image through multiple channels, multiple senses, multiple times. Whatever the need for change is, few people will get it the first time they hear it. In fact, for most people, seeing is not believing, but rather *experiencing* is believing, and experience requires hearing, smelling, touching, tasting, and *seeing*. The key point is that all of us give ourselves far too much credit and forget how many times we had to look at a threat or opportunity, how many different angles we had to explore it, and how long we had to think about it before we finally understood it. Because we forget the process of understanding it, we end up thinking that saying it once to others should be enough and it just isn't—and never will be.

Creating High Contrast and Confrontation

With these two common mistakes in mind, we can now turn our attention to specific means of creating high contrast and confrontation. Because the fundamental principles are relatively straightforward, they only come alive with examples, so we provide several in following pages.

20/80 Rule

Given the tendency to try and paint pictures that are too complicated and comprehensive, effective contrast requires leaders to focus on the core 20 percent. As we already pointed out, reality in its entirety is complex. Left in its full complexity, the important contrasts get lost and are hard to see. Consequently, leaders must simplify and focus on a few key differences. The key here is identifying the *key* differences. Making the judgments as to what are and what are not core contrasts is where great leaders of change distinguish themselves.

To illustrate this, for a moment imagine that you work for the (fictitious) leading signal processing firm, QuadQ, Inc., whose products primarily ship to the healthcare industry. Scientific researchers and hospital researchers use your products in diagnostic tests and in cellular and blood chemical analysis. QuadQ's analog technology has been at the leading edge for years. Then a shift occurs in the market:

- First, digital signal processing emerges as a competing technological platform. When it first emerges, however, it seems unable to rival your analog technology.

- Second, the nature of customers begins to shift. Diagnostics and analyses are done increasingly in clinics and by technicians, not in research labs or large teaching hospitals by MDs and PhDs.

- Third, there is a trend to coordinate separate tests and analyses into integrated diagnostic and testing systems. The emerging "buzz phrase" in your industry becomes "providing solutions, not boxes, to customers."

As signs of these shifts first emerge, many of the scientists within your firm resist the signals that the environment is changing. They work harder at coming up with customized analog solutions for customers. Within a year or two, it becomes increasingly clear to you that digital signal processing is the superior technology in general and specifically for integrating your products into larger solutions. It also becomes more evident to you that digital is the way to go for simplifying the use of your product so that less sophisticated customers can operate the equipment.

How do you create a compelling contrast sufficient to shake your employees free from entrenched mental maps of the glorious past? First, you have to cut to the core. What are the core contrasts between the past and the future? Clearly, QuadQ exists in a very complex environment, but allowing too much of that complexity to creep into the picture can kill employees' ability to see the needed contrast.

While QuadQ's environment is full of complexity, five key contrasts exist: technology, strategy, customers, competencies, and relationships. Keep in mind that as simple as this seems, it still requires people to remember ten things (five categories by two descriptions). You create the matrix illustrated in Table 3.1 to highlight the core contrast.

Table 3.1 The Core of QuadQ's Changing Environment

Issue	Old	New
Technology	Analog	Digital
Strategy	Make leading-edge boxes	Provide leading edge solutions
Customers	Hospital and research centers. Sophisticated doctors and scientists	Clinics and labs Significantly less sophisticated technicians
Key Personal Competencies	Scientific and technical brilliance	Teamwork
Departmental Relations	Autonomous and independent	Collaborative and cooperative

The second thing you do is ratchet up contrast by enhancing the conceptual distance between the descriptions. You know that the reality may not be quite so black and white, but you also know that the greater the contrast, the easier it is for employees to see difference and recognize the acute need for change.

In addition to focusing on the core contrasts, you also take a page from what we know in general about vision and memory. Research has clearly demonstrated that the better you create images (not words) in people's minds, the more clearly they can recall the associated messages. While the matrix in Table 3.1 appeals to your cerebral nature, you realize the need for something else, something more visual. In response, you create a very simple picture that contrasts the old and the new, as illustrated in Figure 3.3.

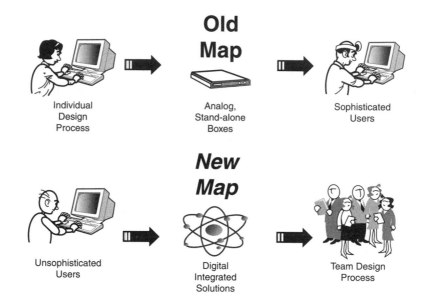

Figure 3.3 QuadQ's old and new map.

Using these images you explain that in the past, individual brilliant scientists created leading-edge analog boxes that very sophisticated customers used. That was the old map. The new map calls for gearing products toward increasingly less sophisticated customers and away from doctors and research scientists. With the new map, QuadQ will create more integrated, digital solutions instead of boxes. Finally, instead of relying on individual brilliance among QuadQ scientists, the future will require cross-functional teams composed of technology, marketing, and manufacturing people to design and produce the new solutions.

To summarize, you take three steps for creating high contrast:

- Focus on the core 20 percent of what is different.
- Enhance (even exaggerate) the differences between the old and new.
- Create visual images, or pictures, of the old and new so that the contrast is understood as more than mere words.

Contrast Enhancement Tool

Because the 20/80 principle is easy to say but hard to do, we have developed a simple tool that helps put this principle into practice. The tool (shown in Table 3.2) is a basic set of questions that uncover common core areas of essential contrast.

Clearly, the questions raised earlier are not the only relevant ones, but our experience is that if people take the time to answer these questions, it nudges their minds enough out of the trap of current mental maps to begin exploring new alternatives. Once people alter the mental terrain, then various contrasts begin to emerge. In fact, typically, once the process starts rolling, lots of contrasts become more visible. At this point in remapping change, the objective is to generate as many potential contrasts as possible for each core area listed in the tool in Table 3.1 (or other areas you see as important to your business that we have not mentioned).

Table 3.2 Contrast Enhancement Tool

Core Area	Key Questions	Critical Contrasts
Customers	Are current customer preferences changing? Are our customers' customers changing? Are new customers emerging?	
Competition	Are competitors changing their value proposition to customers? Are competitors gaining or losing specific competitive advantages? Are new competitors emerging?	
Technology	Are current technologies moving ahead of us? Are potential substitute technologies on the horizon? Are new technologies emerging?	

Table 3.2 Continued

Core Area	Key Questions	Critical Contrasts
Products/Services	Are current product/service offerings changing? Is the value proposition changing? Are new products emerging?	

The next step and task is boiling these contrasts down to the critical few factors—the 20 percent that paint 80 percent of the high contrast picture. Once you have selected these, then you can create a simple matrix (see Table 3.3) that will help others clearly see the most important contrasts.

Table 3.3 Contrast Codification Tool

Core Area	Critical Contrasts	
	Past	Future
Customers		
Competition		
Technology		
Products/Services		

Clearly, pointing out contrasts between the old and new is a critical first step to change. However, to avoid the "I Get It" Mistake, talking through these contrasts just once is not enough. To ensure a high level of confrontation so that the contrast sinks in, you need much more experiential engagement.

An inescapable experience contains two dimensions. The first is (get ready for this) inescapable. By this we mean that the experience is hard for the individual to mentally sidestep or ignore, or to physically walk away from. Second, the experience must be experiential. Again this may sound redundant, but the experience cannot be just mental. It needs to actively involve as many senses as possible—touch, smell, sight, sound, taste. As stated earlier, we know from a wide body of scientific literature that the more senses involved and the deeper their involvement, the higher the impact—more learned and more retained.

To illustrate this, let's return to QuadQ, Inc. As the CEO, you did a good job of creating contrast, but you must also ensure effective confrontation. The message needs repetition—probably more often than you think necessary. In addition, you must create some inescapable experiences. How can you do this? You might borrow a page from the CEO of Samsung Electronics.

Samsung Electronics is a unit within the larger Korean conglomerate. Samsung Electronics is by most accounts the leading consumer electronics company in Korea. It holds the largest market share and a premiere quality image. It was accustomed to operating in a certain way. While things were going fine in Korea, its operations and sales in the U.S. were not going well at all. The CEO was convinced that Samsung had to operate differently in that market than at home, but the message was just not getting through to top managers in Korea. So the CEO created an inescapable experience. He put more than 50 of the most senior executives on a plane, and off they went to visit stores in the U.S.

The contrasts were stark. Rather than being sold in small shops—as in Korea, electronics were sold in large stores in the U.S. Rather than getting prime merchandising space as they did in Korea, Samsung products were in the bargain bin back behind the leaders such as Sony, and even second-tier makers such as Panasonic. Samsung executives saw where their products were displayed, rubbed their fingers across the dust on the products, heard customers talk excitedly about competitors' product features as they shopped, and tasted the envy in their mouth for the position of market leaders in the U.S. Samsung was king at home, but not in the royal court in the U.S.

Samsung executives could not escape the experience. It was repeated essentially a dozen times as the group went from store to store. They could not sidestep the experience because they were physically put in the center of it. As a consequence, the contrast finally delivered deep impact.

As QuadQ's CEO, you should do something similar. You must create an inescapable experience. Simply talking about the contrasts, even repeatedly, is not enough. What can you do? Let's take a look at the Samsung example for key steps.

First, the primary objective of an inescapable experience is putting people directly in front of the most important and forceful aspects of the contrast. As a consequence, you must decide what you want the experience to focus on. Just as there is the danger in diluting the impact of contrast by allowing too much complexity, so too can you dilute the impact of the confronting experience by making it too complex and unfocused. In Samsung's case, what core contrast would hit the executives right between the eyes? It was the treatment of the product. To exaggerate, in Korea Samsung's products are held respectfully in gloved hands when presented to consumers. In the U.S, they're casually tossed into bargain bins with a sign above them reading "Clearance Sale!"

What is the key contrast that can hit QuadQ employees, especially the scientists, right between the eyes? *Customers!* QuadQ scientists are used to interacting with and trying to create sophisticated solutions for other PhD-holding, lab coat-wearing scientist customers. What would happen, though, if you confronted your PhD scientists with a new technician-type customer holding only an associate's degree, sporting purple hair, and wearing a nose ring? On top of that, what would happen if you sat that less-formally educated customer down to run diagnostics on your old analog products and your PhD research scientists were forced to listen to the customer's severe complaints about the products? The new technician-customer is not used to sophisticated "type in" commands but wants drop-down menus and common language vocabulary, not technical jargon. The contrast would be compelling and inescapable. The resulting shock is precisely what your people need for you to have a prayer of overcoming the strength of their old analog map that has dominated the path of success in your firm for the last 40 years.

To summarize, five steps create high impact confrontation:

1. Repeat the messages of the old and new maps *over* and *over* and *over* again.

2. Create high-impact, inescapable confrontations.

3. Focus the experience on what you think are the core contrasts. Do not dilute it with too much complexity.

4. Make sure that the experience involves as many senses as possible. There are few effective substitutes for live, fully-engaged action.

5. Physically ensure that people cannot easily avoid the experience but must take the brunt of it right between the eyes (ears, nose, mouth, and/or hands).

More Examples

Let us provide a couple more real-life examples to further illustrate and reinforce the keys of contrast and confrontation in breaking through the first barrier.

Not long ago a fellow by the name of Tom Alexander was put in charge of a rather large project at Hewlett-Packard. The mandate was to build a $49 printer that could be sold for just under $100 retail. Simple, except that HP's least expensive printer cost them $79 to make. On top of this, the objective was to go from concept to store in three years, or 18 months faster than HP had ever done before. Virtually, all the engineers said, "It can't be done." Why? "We haven't done it before, and if we couldn't do it, who could?" Besides, HP was known for high quality. High quality was in part how they achieved their dominant position in printers. With high quality came higher costs, and so far customers seemed willing to pay the price.

However, Lexmark had introduced a "sub-$100" printer and had seen its share of the market double to 14 percent. Still, some HP engineers reasoned that Lexmark must be selling the printers at a loss because if HP couldn't make a printer for $49, surely Lexmark couldn't either.

How could Tom Alexander produce sufficient contrast and confrontation to break through this barrier and help people see the need for change? How could he both thwart the competitive threat of Lexmark and grab the opportunity for growth? Insightfully, he took an HP printer, put it in the middle the room, and stood on it with his full

200 pounds. What was the contrast? The contrast was a $250 HP "step-stool" printer versus just a printer. After all, how many customers go out thinking, "I don't want a $100 Lexmark printer; I need my $250 HP step-stool printer because you never know when I might need to stand on my printer to reach up to a high shelf?" Yet, what were the associated engineering costs or raw materials going into a printer so rugged that a 200-pound person could stand on it and use it as a step stool? This grandstanding created a brilliant contrast.

How did Tom Alexander create the inescapable confrontation? He stood in silence in the middle of the room. People could see him; they could hear the silence as Tom just stood there; they could almost feel the sturdiness of the printer.

After a few long seconds of standing on the printer in deafening silence, the engineers got it. With that, Tom broke through the first barrier and people could see the need for change. Crazy, you say. Not as crazy as the results. HP subsequently spent $1 billion on the project ($125 million for R&D, $900 million for manufacturing, and $200 million for marketing). The results were spectacular. After the new line of printers came out in 2002, HP took 20 new market share points. In the fourth quarter of 2002, HP saw sales increase 12 percent to $5.6 billion and saw margins increase by nearly 15 percent.

Let's consider one more enlightening example. Throughout the 1990s, the fastest growing and most profitable vehicles in the largest market in the world were full size trucks and SUVs (sport utility vehicles) in the U.S. Executives within Toyota USA saw this and wanted to grasp the opportunity, especially relative to full-size trucks with V8 engines. The executives back in Japan could not see the opportunity. Fundamentally, they felt that the customers for these trucks were construction company workers, ranchers, and farmers—not Toyota's traditional customers. Toyota's main customers were middle-class families. Neither PowerPoint presentations nor Excel spreadsheets helped executives in Japan see the need for change. So how could Toyota executives in the U.S. break through this stubborn brain barrier?

The answer came in the form of an American football. To create the contrast, they took the visiting Japanese headquarter executives to a Dallas Cowboys football game. Anyone who has ever been to a collegiate or professional football game in the U.S. knows what happens for two to three hours before the game ever starts: a tailgate party.

People show up in the parking lot and literally let down the tailgate of their trucks and then barbeque, eat, and party. And who comes in these trucks? In contrast to the Japanese headquarters executives' image of construction workers and ranchers, middle-class families and friends were the ones in the parking lot tailgating. This contrast was driven home by exceptionally high confrontation. By putting the executives in the middle of the tailgate party, they were forced to literally see, hear, touch, smell, and even taste the contrast. There was no way to escape it.

Crazy. But again, not as crazy as the results. During July 1999, the first month that the Tundra was introduced, Toyota sold more than 8,000 units. This was the highest first-month unit sales of any Toyota model ever launched. Since then, sales of have climbed steadily, and Toyota sold more than 127,000 units in 2005. The new and totally redesigned Tundra released in 2007 was expected to reach 200,000 units. While Toyota does not release profits per vehicle figures, Toyota executives will admit that the Tundra is one of its most profitable models on a per-vehicle basis.

Pulling It All Together

Contrast and confrontation are two keys for breaking through the first brain barrier. While we may not have said it explicitly, you no doubt have sensed that changing entrenched mental maps requires a serious shock to the system. In closing, let us make that point clear and unmistakable. The longer a given mental map has been in place and the more successful it has been, the greater the shock needed to break free from it.

As evidence of this consider some personal, managerial maps rather than organizational maps. Most managers grow up in a given country and culture—be that Germany, Australia, Japan, or India. They develop managerial maps of how to successfully communicate, motivate, correct, praise, confront, and direct people. This generally works fine until you must interact effectively with people from multiple countries and cultures. Recently, we conducted a study along with a colleague, Allen Morrison, looking at what experiences helped people develop the abilities to lead effectively in a global environment working with customers, suppliers, and employees from different countries and cultures. When we asked more than 130 senior executives from 55 different companies across Europe, North America, and Asia what the most important and influential experience was in helping them develop global leadership capabilities, 80 percent gave the exact same answer. Given the diversity of these executives (different nationalities, job histories, industries, and so on), this is amazingly high agreement. Eight out of ten executives said an international assignment was the most influential career experience they had. Why?

The following example provides the answer. Not long ago we, along with our colleague Allen Morrison, were on a trip to Japan for an international management conference. Because one of our trio, Stewart Black, had lived and worked in Japan before, he decided to take the other two to a traditional Japanese restaurant for dinner. Being the inter-culturally sensitive guy that he is, he gave the other two a "briefing" about the restaurant and proper etiquette before going in. He explained that most traditional Japanese restaurants have a similar entry. It consists of a thin wood and glass sliding door with an entry area on the other side. The runners at the bottom of the door, along which it slides, are made of wood and are typically not recessed; consequently, he warned the other two that they would need to step carefully over the runners as they enter the restaurant. He then mentioned that they would be in a small alcove called a *genkan* and that they would remove their shoes before stepping up into the restaurant proper.

Once they found what looked like a nice, traditional restaurant, Stewart opened the sliding door and carefully stepped inside. Allen, who is about the same height as Stewart, followed, also being sure to step over the door runners. The next thing anyone knew there was a thunderous crash at the entry that reverberated throughout the entire restaurant. Everyone inside turned to see what had happened. Hal, on seeing his two colleagues negotiate the entry so easily, had tried to step quickly through the door. However, Hal, who is nearly 6'5" (a full 2 meters), smashed his head on the top of the doorframe. The impact nearly knocked out Hal, and the reverberations caused everyone in the restaurant to momentarily wonder if an earthquake were starting.

The most interesting part of this story is that the next day, when the trio went to another traditional Japanese restaurant, the exact same thing happened. Now Hal had a matching bump on the other side of his head. It wasn't until the third time that Hal remembered to duck as he entered. It took getting smacked in the head hard twice for Hal to rearrange his mental map about what it takes for him to enter a traditional Japanese restaurant successfully.

Most of us are like Hal. It takes getting smacked in the head, hard and probably more than once, before we are ready to rearrange what is in our heads—our mental maps. Hard knocks to the head are not always pleasant—in fact they hurt—but they are necessary.

International assignments, unlike short trips, almost always result in some serious smacks to the head. On international assignments, on a daily basis we confront managerial situations in which our old maps do not work. Because we cannot easily hide out in our hotel room for three years, we eventually smack our heads—hard and usually repeatedly. This head-smacking is what caused the global leaders we interviewed to change their managerial mental maps. And this is why eight out of ten global executives touted an international assignment as the most important developmental experience in their career.

The point is not that everyone should go on an international assignment (though if you want to be a global leader, you should seriously consider it). Rather, the point is to illustrate that a smack in the head with contrast and confrontation is usually needed to dislodge entrenched mental maps. These smacks help us see that our mental maps have limits and help us deal with shifts in the environment. In the end, we must stretch and rearrange our maps—as painful as that might be.

Barrier #2: Failure to Move

In the previous chapter, we voted you in as CEO of QuadQ, Inc., the signal processing firm. We now want to return you to that role. Recall that your products primarily go to the healthcare industry, and in the past they were used by scientific and hospital researchers in diagnostic tests as well as cellular and blood chemical analysis. Your analog technology has defined the leading edge for years. However, the technology has shifted from analog to digital, the market from sophisticated customers to technicians, and products from stand-alone boxes to integrated solutions.

Finally, after articulating the core contrasts and confronting key scientists with an inescapable encounter with the new type of customer, most technical and scientific personnel in your firm capitulate. They throw their arms up and exclaim, "Digital signal processors are the future." Their old mental maps of how the world works are broken. Your matrix, your pictures, and even your customer experience all produced their intended effect. You even polished your vision speech:

Folks, we are facing a brave new world. Technology is shifting from analog to digital signal processing. Our strategy and competitive advantage have always been and will remain our leading edge technology. We must embrace this new technology. In addition, our customers are shifting from hospitals, sophisticated doctors and research scientists to clinics and technicians. With this shift in customers, our products must become more "user-friendly" and simpler to operate. Furthermore, we cannot afford to simply make boxes. We must provide more integrated solutions. To accomplish this, we must work more in cross-functional teams. We need R&D, engineering, marketing, and sales to work together so that we fully incorporate changing customers' needs into the design of our products from the start. In addition, speed to market will be critical to our future success, which will require greater coordination and cooperation across various departments. **Simpler, speedier solutions!** This is the vision!

You followed this book's advice (good move), and you communicated, communicated, and communicated the vision—the new map. You sent out emails; you made a couple of short videos for broadcast during lunches in the company dining room; you made several PowerPoint presentations to different groups and departments. You kept your message consistent and concise.

Now you sit back and wait to see the inevitable change within your company. You wait and you wait and you wait. Nothing changes; no one moves. What's up?

You're perplexed. You've broken through the first barrier and people see the need for change. If they see that the old right thing is now wrong and that digital signal processing is the future, why aren't they moving in that direction? You just don't get it. After all, you read the first three chapters of this book and followed our advice. People now not only see that the old right thing is now wrong, but they also have a clear idea of what the new right thing is, right? You have made the vision clear. Oddly, you begin to feel as though the clearer you make the vision and the more you repeat it, the more resistance to movement you begin to feel.

Why aren't people moving?

This illustrates the second powerful barrier against change: *failure to move.* For most people we talk with, the first barrier to change makes more intuitive sense than the second. Most people understand quite easily that if people don't see the need for change, they are unlikely to change. But if people begin to see the need for change, why would they fail to move? After all, not jumping out of the way of a truck heading right for you because you didn't see it is one thing. But failing to move after you see the truck bearing down on you is quite another. Are people who see the need, but still fail to move, just plain stupid?

In our experience, people who fail to move even after they see the need are quite *smart*, not stupid. To understand clearly why we say this and why they fail to move even when they see the need, we need to break the second barrier into two parts.

The first part involves the distinction between seeing that the old right thing is now wrong and seeing the new right thing. The first does not necessarily lead to the second. That is, just because someone finally capitulates and admits that the old right thing is wrong does not mean that they see the new right thing. Because of this, people will fail to move if the new right thing is not clear.

Consider Xerox. It has had a history of doing the right thing and doing it well. Early in its history, it focused on making copiers for businesses. They were big and expensive and made the company tons of money. Unfortunately for them, the environment shifted. The right thing ended up being the wrong thing. For example, Canon came along and introduced the personal copier for a price that was one-tenth the cost of Xerox's low-end machines. At first, Xerox denied the shift in the market until it was almost too late. Xerox viewed personal copiers as a novelty item instead of a serious business line. Early on, the company even refused to leverage a personal copier that its joint venture with Fuji (FujiXerox) created in Japan. Finally, Xerox responded and regained a respectable position in the personal copier segment. Yet in the mid-1990s, Xerox once again faced the challenge of change.

To tackle this transformation, Rick Thoman—a key player in IBM's dramatic turnaround—was brought onboard. When he came to Xerox, he laid out a principal vision that was quite similar to the vision that successfully transformed IBM in the early 1990's—a new map that propelled IBM's stock price from near $40 to $200 (split adjusted) by that point. (It later reached a high of just over $400.) IBM's vision demanded solutions (not just boxes) for customers through global ISUs (Industry Solution Units). The fundamental notion at IBM was that customer solutions within a given industry would be more similar than solutions across industries. In other words, a solution for Citigroup would be more similar to a solution for HSBC than a solution for Shell. IBM determined that firms' needs within a given industry (such as banks) were more similar to each other than they were to firms in other industries.

IBM's strategy and structure were designed to not just make sense, but to make money. The view was that if IBM could utilize 50-70 percent of a solution it had created for Citigroup for HSBC as well, it could extract significant margins. After all, Citigroup would have already paid full price for the solution IBM developed for it. IBM would then charge HSBC full price, but in one sense, part of the solution for HSBC would have already paid for. In many ways the new strategy and structure worked wonderfully, and "services" became a major source of IBM's revenue and profit growth during the mid to late 1990s.

As the new CEO, Thoman delivered a similar vision to Xerox. Customers needed document solutions, not just copiers. Customers grouped by industry would have more similar needs and therefore require more similar solutions than customers grouped by geography (territories). This constituted the new map for a new Xerox.

However, the mental maps for many Xerox employees were radically different. Xerox sales and service organizations had been organized largely by geographic territory in the past. As a consequence, Xerox sales people knew customers within their sales territory well, regardless of what industry they were in. Yet, as deteriorating financial results mounted and Xerox stock price fell into a near free fall, evidence piled up that the old way was just not right anymore. Thus, the old "geographic sales" and "copiers" map began to crumble, making way for a new "document solutions" map.

Still, people within Xerox failed to change. Why? Why did people fail to move when it became crystal clear that what used to work in the past didn't work at all in the present? As we already mentioned, remember that even if we see that the old right thing no longer works, we still don't move if the new map with its destination and path is not clear. After all, how reasonable is it to venture out into the dark and unknown just because it feels a bit uncomfortable where you are sitting today? And as strange as it may seem, even if we can no longer deny and must admit that the old right thing is now wrong, when lacking a new right direction, we often simply intensify our efforts at doing what we know.

Terrific. But Rick Thoman did deliver his new vision for Xerox. He presented the vision, strategy, and new structure clearly and repeatedly to Xerox employees. Yet in this case (and many others that we have witnessed), people still failed to move. In fact, people so dramatically failed to move at Xerox that Thoman was forced out of the company less than two years after assuming the helm.

Let's take a minute and recap. First, we pointed out that even when people see that the old right thing is now wrong, they fail to move if they do not see the new right thing. Second, as we illustrated with the Xerox's example, even when people finally acknowledge the need for change and even see the new direction, they often still fail to move.

Of the two parts, the second is clearly the more perplexing. After all, it is one thing for people to fail to move if they recognize the need but are not given a new direction to march in, but it is quite another for people to fail to move even after the new vision is clearly presented and understood.

But the most perplexing and paradoxical thing we have consistently observed is that quite often the *clearer* the new vision, the more **im**mobilized employees become. How can this be? We just argued in the previous two chapters that leaders must create in people a recognized need for change and then show them the new direction. How can it be that often—actually, all too often—the clearer the vision and new map the more immobilized people become? Again the question is: Are they stupid?

Our experience is that this happens because people are smart, not stupid. So, how can *not* moving be smart even when it is clear that the old right thing is now wrong? How can not moving be smart when the new right thing is brilliantly illuminated? It is smart because people recognize that there are two sides to the story. The first side focuses on the "right thing" and the "wrong thing." The second emphasizes "doing things well" and "doing things poorly" as Figure 4.1 reminds us.

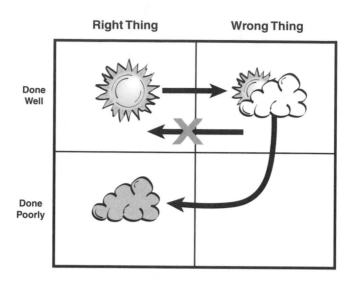

Right Thing   **Wrong Thing**

Done
Well

Done
Poorly

Figure 4.1 Change matrix.

People recognize that they cannot go directly and instantly from doing the old wrong thing well to doing the new right thing well. They understand that they will go from doing the *wrong* thing *well* to doing the *right* thing *poorly*. Given this brilliant insight, imagine from their perspective how silly a leader shouting for change might seem. Essentially, from their perspective the leader is saying, "Follow me and you will do the right thing and you will do it POORLY!" How appealing is that? Yet even if the leader has no intention of communicating this message, people know that is exactly what is going to happen. They are so smart that even if you don't see it or even if you try and hide it, they are not fooled.

No one expects to be instantly great at something they have not done before. This is part of the reason that we don't take up new languages, sports, musical instruments, and so on with greater frequency. Most of us do not like to be bad at something, especially if we are already good at something else.[1]

---

[1] Of course, some people relish the challenge of learning new skills, and these folks are often the first to move after seeing the need for change. However, they usually constitute the minority, not the majority, when confronted with major organizational change.

That is why for most people, going from being competent to incompetent is a very unappealing proposition. Ironically, this is also why the clearer the vision of the new right thing, the more immobilized people often become. The clearer the new vision, the easier it is for people to see all the specific ways in which they will be incompetent and look stupid—ways that they will do the right thing and do it poorly.

For example, let's once again put you back in as CEO of our signal processing company, QuadQ, Inc. At first, the company's performance began to deteriorate because people were trapped in old mental maps of success. As evidence mounted and you provided the needed contrast and confrontation, employees began to see that the old right thing was now wrong. Even with this recognition, though, they failed to move at first because they could not see the new direction—the future vision was not clear. This makes sense. No one wants to take a walk in the dark. Then you clearly illuminated the future vision and map. Yet the more clarity you added, the easier it was for people to see and anticipate what they were going to soon be terrible at (because they are smart).

Consider the scientists and engineers in the firm who had made their careers in analog technology. As the digital future became clearer, so did their visions of their future incompetency. As readers with backgrounds or exposure to these two disciplines know, moving from analog to digital as a scientist or engineer is not an overnight process. In many ways, it is like having learned Chinese and then being told to pick up Greek over a long weekend. Yes, both are languages, and having learned one, you may have developed some general language learning capabilities, but learning Greek from a Chinese base is almost like starting over. In fact, the clearer the differences between the Chinese you know and the Greek that you do not, the easier it is for you to anticipate how difficult it will be to learn Greek and how bad you will be at speaking it. You can easily imagine how many mistakes of grammar, pronunciation, usage, and so on you will make. You can see a movie in your mind's eye of how dumb you will look trying to speak Greek and how smart you look when speaking Chinese. The clearer the images of how dumb you will look making these mistakes, the less you want to move toward learning Greek. Back at QuadQ, the more the scientists and engineers saw that digital signal processors were the future, the more they saw how bad they were going to be—how incompetent at the new right thing they were going to look.

The same dynamic applies to many other aspects of the new vision. Your scientists and engineers had made their careers through technical brilliance as star individuals. In fact, in the past knowledge of or experience with "inferior" departments, such as marketing, was definitely a negative—not a positive. (By the way, your QuadQ scientists didn't even dignify areas such as marketing or sales by calling them disciplines; they called them functions, not disciplines.) The new vision makes it clear that working in cross-functional teams will be required for success in the future. Clearly this calls for some understanding of what other functions would do. What do these scientists know about working in cross-functional teams? Nothing. What do they know about working on even technical teams to deliver integrated solutions? Nothing. How good at teams in general, and in cross-functional teams in particular, will they be? Terrible. The scientists and engineers could see this. The clearer you made the vision, the more you repeated it, the easier it was for your scientists to see how bad they would be at the new right thing. What did they do? They resisted. Why? Because after a life devoted to being brilliant, they did not want to look stupid.

The same dynamic was true at Xerox. The clearer the vision about solutions and ISUs, the easier it was for sales people to see how bad they were going to be at the new right thing. After all, what did they know about delivering solutions? Nothing. What did they know about working in industry-focused teams? Nothing. Consequently, how good were they likely to be at it? Terrible. Because they were smart, not dumb, they did not want to look or feel stupid. Add to this mix a culture in which mistakes were often punished and learning was rarely rewarded, and you must wonder: Who would want to venture off into the land of certain incompetence and probable punishment when they could stay at home where demonstrated capabilities were respected? No one.

Some might argue that the vision, strategy, and structure that Thoman brought to Xerox were wrong for the company, that Thoman inappropriately just took what he knew and what had worked at IBM and forced it on Xerox. Perhaps. It is hard to know for sure. (Though the current CEO, Anne Mulcahy, is pursuing a similar strategy.) Many thought the vision, strategy, and structure that Gerstner (with Thoman's help) implemented at IBM were wrong until they began to work. Perhaps those who thought the vision, strategy, and structure that Thoman brought to Xerox were wrong would be singing a different tune if they had delivered results. Our main point is that the vision might have worked if Xerox employees had actually seen a path from doing the right thing poorly to doing it well. In other words, many preferred to be *competent at the wrong thing* than *incompetent at the right thing*. As long as they saw a future filled with doing the right thing poorly, most employees were not inclined to move. Our point is that movement was unlikely until employees plainly saw a promising path to the promised land.

While the details of creating a "promising path" is a key focus of the next chapter (Chapter 5, "Solutions and Tools for Breaking through Barrier #2: Helping People Make the Move"), the point we want to stress here is that people fail to move even when they see the need because most will do just about anything to avoid doing the new right thing and doing it poorly. Not only do people need to see the new direction or destination, they must see, and more importantly, *believe* in a path that will take them from doing the right thing poorly to doing it well. Without this prospect, many people prefer competence at the wrong thing to incompetence at the right one.

As mentioned earlier, most change books and change consultants harp on the need to provide a vision of the future—a new direction or destination. We agree. Most of us are not too keen on venturing out into the dark, especially if there is a safe light still on where we are. On this point, we are reminded of the old joke about a man who lost his ring. He searches madly for it, and along comes a stranger asking, "What did you lose?" "My ring," he replies. "Where did you lose it?" asks the passerby. "Way over there," the man frantically answers. "Then why are you looking here?" queries the intended helper. "Because this is where the light is," replies the hopeless searcher. In organizations, people also stay where the light is even when they recognize it is the wrong place. People often stick to what they are good at, even when they see it has become irrelevant.

Pulling It All Together

To summarize, two keys make it possible to overcome the second barrier to change. First, even after we have helped people see that the old right thing is now wrong, and we have painted a picture of the new right thing, that new map must have a clear destination or vision. The map must answer the question, "Where are we going?" Yet this is not enough. In fact, the clearer the answer to where we are going, the greater the resistance to getting there because people can now see how bad they will look doing the new right thing. Consequently, along with illuminating the new right thing, we must create a belief in people that new maps contain a promising path that will guide them through doing the new right thing poorly to doing it very well.

In our experience it is this part of the second change barrier that receives far too little managerial attention, and yet it is really responsible for most resistance to change. Even if people see the new right thing, they must also see a way to travel from doing the right thing poorly to doing it well. How to paint inspiring and illuminating new visions as well as promising paths to the promised land fills the next chapter.

5

five

Solutions and Tools for Breaking through Barrier #2: Helping People Make the Move

When we last left you as CEO of QuadQ, you had succeeded in creating sufficient contrast and confrontation for people to see that their old maps were plain wrong, and you created a clear image of the new destination. However, the clearer you made the vision, the more QuadQ's people resisted in moving to make the change. Having read the previous chapter, you now understand why. Your people know that traveling to the new destination will require that they stop doing the wrong thing quite competently and start doing the new right thing quite incompetently. Now they must not only see the new destination, but you must help them come to believe in a path that will take them from doing the new right thing poorly to doing it well. Without this fundamental belief in a path and their individual abilities to follow it, they will refuse to move—in spite of an obvious and compelling need and destination.

Helping others gain this belief requires three key steps:

1. Making sure they see the destination or target clearly.
2. Giving them the skills, resources, and tools necessary to reach the destination.
3. Delivering valuable rewards to them along the journey.

These steps emerge from one of the most tested and validated theories in human psychology and management—expectancy theory. While we do not want to waste your time with the detailed in's and out's of the theory, we mention it for two reasons. First, what we present is not just our thoughts or opinions, but is supported by scores and scores of published research. Second, while we generated many ideas for this book, we do not want credit where it is not due. As PhD students, we studied under one of the principal architects of expectancy theory. Put simply, while expectancy theory is not our idea, it has powerful application in overcoming the second barrier for change—failure to move.

Step 1: Destination

Because we already mentioned this issue in the previous chapter, we will be brief here. Just as it is difficult to motivate someone to shoot at an unclear target, it is equally difficult to motivate employees to take off in search of a fuzzy destination. If the destination is not clear, what is the chance of arriving there? If the chance of arriving it is low, how high is your motivation to try? The answers to these questions are obvious. If the direction and destination are not clear, your motivation to move forward is nil. As a consequence, you will not be surprised to learn that more than 100 research studies have confirmed this.

A key, practical step in establishing effective targets is translating the vision of the new right thing into concrete behaviors. For example, if "Customer 1st" is the new vision, what will that look like in terms of behavior? How would you recognize "Customer 1st" behavior if you saw it? For example, let's take the case of Sam, an airline gate agent. The CEO has announced and explained the new "Customer 1st" vision. What does this mean for Sam in real life? Table 5.1 provides a tool we use with managers in clarifying the new right thing in terms of concrete behaviors for the employees they want to get moving.

As a side point, the more complex the new right thing, the more important it is to define the key situations and the associated concrete behaviors that, for employees, constitute the essence of the new right thing. Fancy phrases like "Customer 1st" mean very little to a gate agent, and they mean even less to a customer if the gate agent's behavior is no different than it was before the change initiative.

For example, in Sam's case one of the most common situations for making the vision of "Customer 1st" a reality happens when someone arrives late to the gate. Another common situation occurs when flights are delayed or cancelled. The tool in Table 5.1 can help you define key situations in your change initiative that matter to the employee and then describe in detail the relevant desired behaviors.

Table 5.1 Tool for Translating the New Right Thing into Behaviors

Common Situation	Targeted Behaviors
A.	1.
	2.
	3.
B.	1.
	2.
	3.
C.	1.
	2.
	3.

For example, when a customer arrives late at the gate, one concrete behavior of the new "Customer 1st" vision for Sam is empathizing with customer frustration at missing flights. "Sir, I can imagine that it is frustrating to have hurried here and then arrived too late to catch the flight." Another behavior is proactively working to help the customer get to his destination. "Our next flight to London is in 40 minutes, and on that flight I believe I can even get you an exit row seat with a little more leg room if you like." Only when targets are this concrete and clear will Sam move forward.

While this approach to change may seem detailed, we have noticed two important implications in our research and work with clients:

- First, without clear and concrete target behaviors, most people will not move. So while it may take a bit of time and effort to detail the most common situations and describe the targeted behaviors, the negative returns for not doing it compared to the positive returns for the time and effort for doing it make the decision to invest an easy one.

● Second, we have discovered that if you focus on the 20 percent of situations—and related target behaviors—that cover 80 percent of the new vision, the rest of the less-core situations and behaviors take care of themselves.

What do we mean that the rest take care of themselves? To illustrate, return to Sam our airline gate agent. For Sam, two situations—customers arriving late and delayed (or cancelled) flights—are within the critical core 20 percent that account for 80 percent of all customer service situations. By knowing what the targeted behaviors are for these core situations, Sam can "fill in the blanks" reasonably well on his own about "Customer 1st" behaviors for less common situations. That is, as Sam encounters the other less common situations, he can reasonably extrapolate from the identified core situations and make reasonably sound judgments as to what the targeted behaviors should be. The implication of this point is critical. If you take the time and invest the resources to identify the core 20 percent situations and describe the related target behaviors, you will not need to make the same resource investment in the remaining 80 percent; you will have equipped your people to do that job for you.

The tool we provide in Table 5.1 is fairly direct, and some readers may believe that their subordinates will find it too pedestrian. Fair enough. However, the underlying principle still applies. That is, unless people see the implications of the new right thing concretely for themselves, they are unlikely to make the needed changes, and the needed changes always show up in behaviors. Therefore, if Table 5.1 is too pedestrian for your folks, skip it and simply ask them what the implications of the new destination are for them. Ask them what the new destination will require from them in terms of personal capabilities. If the old map involved walking along the beach and the new one requires a trek up a mountain, anyone who sees the difference will surely recognize the need for boots on the mountain trek where bare feet might have been perfectly fine on the beach.

For example, the CEO of a large oil company laid out a new strategic map that demanded a shift from independent and autonomous business units to more interdependent and coordinated units. If his vision was clear enough, company executives should be able communicate back to the CEO a solid grasp of how all the firm's value chain activities fit together. Furthermore, they should be able to explain how they will need better conflict resolution skills because they won't any longer be able to simply go their own way if they have differences of opinion. If the CEO's direct reports can't see some of these implications and required capabilities on their own, odds are that the target is not yet clear enough.

Step 2: Resources

Once the destination is clear in employees' minds, the key question then becomes whether people believe they have what it takes to walk the path and reach the promised land. Scaling a tall peak can sound great, unless we don't believe we have the gear (ropes, boots, harness) we need, the skills required, or the mandated physical strength. Quite simply, if people believe they do not have what it takes to walk the path and reach the destination, they are not motivated to try. If they do have it, they are. But once again, what idiot leader among us would ask employees to scale a mountain for which they had neither the necessary gear nor capabilities? By definition, if we give them a mountain to climb, we believe they have what it takes to make it.

As in Step 1, the key to Step 2 lies in realizing that *our* assessments do not matter. In the final analysis *it is what employees believe that counts.* If they do not believe, then they will not try (or at least will not try very hard). If they do believe, they will at least try. While we as leaders must make our assessments as to what the required tools and capabilities are, the real challenge lies in determining if employees believe they possess what it takes, and helping them to believe if they do not.

A brief personal example may be helpful here. Several years ago one of us (Stewart) managed a consulting firm in Japan. In that position, one of Stewart's responsibilities was a new product launch. He made the destination clear to the salesmen (all were men). They all clearly saw the sales target. Stewart then put together a compelling reward package. Salesmen saw the target clearly and wanted the promised rewards, yet the launch went nowhere—no sales prospects emerged.

Why? In some private conversations after work, Stewart was told that none of the salesmen had mentioned the new product to a single client. No mention of the new product generally leads to no sales prospects. Why wasn't the product mentioned? Because the salesmen were good at their jobs, they imagined how a sales call might go—what they would say, what a client might ask, how they would answer, and so on. In doing so, they all envisioned that clients might ask a few questions for which they did not have the answers. That would be embarrassing, which was unacceptable in a Japanese context. To avoid the potential embarrassment, they simply avoided the situation by not mentioning the new product.

What was missing? The target was clear. The rewards were motivating. The salesmen had the selling capabilities. The resource they lacked was a bit of information with which they could answer some tough questions. Stewart thought they had this knowledge. (To be honest, he thought he had provided it in his presentation—clearly a victim of the "I get it" trap.) Stewart did not check to see that the salesmen believed they had the information. All it took was their believing that they did *not* have the resource (or, the knowledge that would answer certain customer questions), and they didn't even attempt to make the trip down this new product path despite it being clear and highly rewarded.

To fully support movement, we use the following tool in Table 5.2 to help map out the full spectrum of required resources. This tool also helps you identify the necessary actions to supply your people with needed resources so that they can individually bridge the gap between what they have and what they need.

Table 5.2 Tool for Mapping Out Required Resources

Capabilities			
Old	**New**	**Gap**	**Bridge**
1.		Small Medium Large	1. 2.
2.		Small Medium Large	1 2.
3.		Small Medium Large	1. 2.
4.		Small Medium Large	1. 2.
5.		Small Medium Large	1. 2.
6.		Small Medium Large	1. 2.

Knowledge			
Old	New	Gap	Bridge
1.		Small Medium Large	1. 2.
2.		Small Medium Large	1. 2.
3.		Small Medium Large	1. 2.
4.		Small Medium Large	1. 2.
5.		Small Medium Large	1. 2.
6.		Small Medium Large	1. 2.

Other Resources			
Old	New	Gap	Bridge
1.		Small Medium Large	1. 2.
2.		Small Medium Large	1. 2.
3.		Small Medium Large	1. 2.
4.		Small Medium Large	1. 2.
5.		Small Medium Large	1. 2.
6.		Small Medium Large	1. 2.

Once you have determined the required capabilities, then you must build those capabilities in your people. This is what goes under the "bridge" column in the tool in Table 5.2. The bridge to close the gap between where employees are and where they need to be may involve substantial training, education, experience, mentoring, coaching, or any number of other techniques to generate the essential capabilities for mastering the new right things demanded from your change initiative.

In Step 2, employees essentially ask the question "If I try, can I do it?" If the answer is no (no matter how clear the target), people will fail to move. As leaders, our job in Step 2 is to ensure that they believe they have the right resources.

Step 3: Rewards

Step 1 ensured that the destination was clear in employees' minds, and Step 2 formed a belief in employees that they had the resources to walk the path and reach the promised land. Step 3 involves the most familiar aspect of getting people to move—rewards. All of us know the power of rewards in motivating and moving people.

When we think of rewards, many of us think of money. No question, money is a motivating reward for most people. However, it is not the only motivating reward, and it is not nearly as powerful as we often suppose. To put money in its proper place as a reward, we must appreciate two important things.

First, money is often a means to something else that people care about. Money buys a college education for a child. Money buys a new car when the old one is breaking down. Money also buys a new car and boosts one's ego. Money buys a vacation to take a break from earning more money. For many people, money is a necessary means to what they truly value—security, ego, status, friendship, health, fun, and so on. However, as we discover what people really care about, we may also identify alternative means (instead of money) to fulfill those needs. For example, employees who are driven by status may find a visible assignment much more rewarding than money. For people who really value fun, a company party may deliver the goods. The point is that many things matter much more to people than money, and money is often just a means to what really matters to them anyway. If we can identify what others' truly desire, we may well take a different (and often more direct) route to help them fulfill it.

The second thing to keep in mind about money is that its effects are often much less powerful than we believe. For example, a yearly bonus (if it is large enough) can be a very powerful incentive for most people. Yet, if the daily reinforcement employees receive from each other and from their leaders is contrary to the year-end bonus scheme, which reward exerts more power? You may find it surprising, but research has clearly established that in most cases the immediate and repeated reinforcements people receive are much more powerful than once-a-year bonuses. The point here is not to abolish annual bonuses, but simply to recognize that bonuses paid out more frequently, along with daily praise, recognition, complements, and so on, are much more compelling reinforcements than once-a-year experiences.

How do you figure out what people really value? Do you just go up to them as ask, "Hey, what do you really value? What makes you tick? Tell me so that I can press the right buttons to motivate you and get you moving?" Of course you don't. While we think we have a framework to help you investigate what people value, there is no shortcut or "one-minute" solution here. People are not human vending machines with personal values prominently displayed for any prospective bidder who inserts the right change and pushes the right buttons. Instead, discovering what other individuals deeply value and care about demands significant time and sincere effort. Period.

People can value almost anything. If you used the process of elimination, it might take decades to eliminate all the secondary and tertiary values and zero in on a person's core values. If you want to come in out of the cold in terms of understanding others' motivation, consider using the *ARCTIC approach* (Achievement, Relations, Conceptual/Thinking, Improvement, and Control).

The ARCTIC approach represents major categories of values (some scholars call them *needs*) that people exhibit from a motivational perspective. Each one has two related sub-dimensions, as summarized in Table 5.3.

While we may all exhibit these needs or values to some extent or another, research has clearly demonstrated, and no doubt your own personal experience verifies, that the strength of these needs varies from person to person. Why they vary is the subject of countless books and debates. That question is really not relevant here. What is important is that if we want to move people to a new destination, we must ensure that the prize for following the new path is motivating to each individual.

Consider just one short sentence uttered by one of the authors (Hal) and see if you can zero in on what motivates him. Just before a recent round-the-world trip, Hal commented to his wife, "I'm really excited to travel to Ireland and discover more about where our ancestors lived." Using the ARTIC framework, what motivates Hal? If you look through the list, one item jumps out more than the others—Improvement, and in particular Exploration. The point is that if you listen carefully to others, they provide a constant stream of clues as to what they really care about and therefore what you can use to really motivate them.

Table 5.3   ARCTIC Framework of Needs

Achievement	
Accomplishment:	The need to meet or beat goals, to do better in the future than one has done in the past.
Competition:	The need to compare one's performance to that of others and do better than they do.
Relations	
Approval:	The need to be appreciated and recognized by others.
Belonging:	The need to feel a part of and accepted by the group.
Conceptual/Thinking	
Problem-Solving:	The need to confront problems and create answers.
Coordination:	The need to relate pieces and integrate them into a whole.
Improvement	
Growth:	The need to feel continued improvement and growth as a person, not just improved results.
Exploration:	The need to move into unknown territory for discovery.
Control	
Competence:	The need to feel personally capable and competent.
Influence:	The need to influence others' opinions and actions.

For some, the motivating prize will be the chance for serious competition. For others, highlighting competition would simply paralyze them with fear, and instead we might stress the personal growth opportunities that a new path presents. The key is listening and identifying the most powerful motivators for a given individual.

We use the tool in Table 5.4 to help with this diagnosing and planning process for individuals. We start by identifying who the key individuals are to motivate and move. In every organization or sub-unit, we always find key informal leaders and trendsetters. Quite often if you can get them moving, others follow. Next, we go through each of the motivation areas and sub-areas on the tool below and determine which we believe are the top three most powerful in motivating that specific individual. Finally, for each of the top three areas we write out a few concrete actions that can be taken to motivate the person. Again, while this is a significant investment of time and energy, the negative consequences of not doing it and the positive payoffs of spending the time and effort make it a step you can't afford to skip.

Table 5.4   ARCTIC Framework of Individual Analysis

Key Individual: _____			
Area	**Sub-Area**	**Top 3**	**Action**
Achievement	Accomplishment	YES NO	1. 2.
	Competition	YES NO	1. 2.
Relations	Approval	YES NO	1. 2.
	Belonging	YES NO	1. 2.
Conceptual/ Thinking	Problem-Solving	YES NO	1. 2.
	Coordination	YES NO	1. 2.
Improvement	Growth	YES NO	1. 2.
	Exploration	YES NO	1. 2.
Control	Competence	YES NO	1. 2.
	Influence	YES NO	1. 2.

Astute readers who face large-scale change initiatives will no doubt be thinking, "This is all well and good, but I have hundreds of people I need to get moving. I can't afford to get to know them all and provide customized, individual rewards." Moving many people at once is a challenge, but our point is that if you cannot get individuals to move, then the masses won't either. The trick is to cascade this individualization of understanding and reward customization down through the organization. You learn what your people really value, and customize the prizes you pass out for following the path to change. Then your direct reports do the same and customize rewards for their people, and so on down the line.

By the way, the higher you are in your organization, the more—not less—important being able to motivate individuals actually becomes in making change happen. Here's why. Typically, the higher we go in the organizational hierarchy, the more convinced we become of our power and authority. After all, as CEO or as some other senior executive, when we call people they get right back to us; people change calendars to meet our schedule; when we shout "jump," people ask "how high?" on the way up. However, keep in mind that the higher you go, the more other people outnumber you. No matter what you declare to shareholders or the media about a marvelous new strategic initiative, if all those people below you don't move as individuals, the entire organization doesn't move either.

Pulling It All Together

Successfully getting people to move encompassed several key points. First, people fail to see the need for change because the mental maps already in their heads blind them. If you can't change these maps, change will go nowhere. However, even if you get people to recognize that what was once right is now wrong, they still may not move. In other words, while overcoming the first barrier to change is necessary, it is not sufficient. Change initiatives can and often do fail because people fail to move even when they see the need. And they fail to move because they do not see or believe in the new path, their ability to walk it, or that the journey and destination will be rewarding. Consequently, they would rather remain quite competent at doing the old wrong thing than incompetent at doing the new right thing.

For people to really get moving, they must clearly see in their own minds—not ours—where they are going. They must *believe* they have the required resources to walk the path and reach the promised land. And they must believe that outcomes they value will come their way if they follow the path outlined by the new map and reach the desired destination. The key thing to remember here is that *their* belief that all three components are in place counts—*not yours.* If *they* don't see it and believe it, nothing else really matters.

We wish this were the end of the story, but it's not. In the next chapter, we examine why, despite seeing and believing, many people still fail to finish and get tripped up by the last barrier to leading strategic change.

6
s i x

Barrier #3: Failure to Finish

Returning to our flight metaphor, at this point you have pushed the throttle forward, and your 100-ton change project begins to lumber down the runway. You build up speed until you reach the point where people recognize that the old right thing is now wrong. You continue to build momentum until you pass the critical point where you need more runway to stop than to take off. People now see what the new right thing is. You celebrate a little; you have overcome the first barrier to change.

As you continue down the runway, your airspeed climbs until you reach that magical point of "rotation," where the plane's speed is sufficient to pull back on the "stick" and lift up the nose. Then the friction and noise of the tires on the tarmac disappear as you break free from the earth. Now people not only see the new right thing, but they believe in the path that will enable them to go from doing the new right thing poorly to doing it well. You celebrate a bit more; you have overcome the second barrier to change. You are airborne.

Given all the energy it takes to get off the ground, it should be smooth flying from here, right? By some rules of fairness, it should be, but anyone with any experience in leading change knows that some of the toughest aspects of change are yet to come. Like a plane, while the runout and even liftoff are necessary for flight, all it takes is a bit of a throttle-back on the power and the plane will come crashing back to the ground. Despite breaking the bonds of earth, gravity still exerts its invisible power, waiting for the opportunity to pull flights of fancy back into its crushing embrace.

Thus, even after overcoming the initial forces of gravity and the two barriers to change—Failure to See and Failure to Move—the third powerful barrier remains: the Failure to Finish. This force silently, patiently, and persistently waits for any opportunity to demonstrate its destructive power. Consequently, successful change must also overcome the third barrier if ultimate success is to be achieved.

Whether the focus of the transformation is on quality, innovation, customer service, speed, or globalization, the full impact and benefits of the "organizational" change cannot be realized until the majority of "individuals" change. Quite simply, new transformational strategies do not make a difference until people think and act differently. Historically, as we have already pointed out, people do not change easily or quickly. When you have an organizational change that involves thousands of individuals, it is impossible to implement the change overnight; instead, it takes months and months, if not years. It takes time for the desired changes to ripple through the organization. One consequence of this time lag is the significant risk that people will get tired and lost during the interim. These two principle forces hold organizations back from moving fast enough or going far enough in their change.

Getting Tired

People get tired because organizational transformation is fundamentally not about transforming the organization; it is about transforming the people who work in it. Certain aspects of the organization, its strategy, structure, or systems can and often do need to be transformed. However, have you ever seen a transformational strategy make a long-term difference when the individuals in the company did not have to transform their thinking and behavior? Have you ever seen a new structure work when the people in that structure did not change their thoughts and actions? The answer is "No." The "rubber" of change meets the "road" of results in people's behaviors. If the people themselves don't change, the wheels spin, and the strategic initiative gets zero traction.

For example, an airline can decide that its new strategy and culture will focus on putting the customer first, as British Airlines (BA) did a few years ago. BA even implemented a program called "Customer 1st." BA can create a new mission statement; it can put out a thousand press releases; it can put up a million "Customer 1st" banners in airports all around the world; but customers only experience and respond to the change when ticket agents, reservation agents, flight attendants, and ground personnel actually put the customer first. Until then, it is all just corporate peacock feathers.

This is not to say that organizational elements, such as incentives or information systems, do not have an impact on people and their behaviors. Clearly they can and do. For example, people act on the information they have, so information systems matter because of the type, quality, and speed of information they deliver to people. The point is not to say that systems do not matter. Rather, in the final analysis what really matters in organizational transformations is the change in people's behaviors and how systems either enhance or detract from that.

Unfortunately, too often this simple fundamental is forgotten, or at least temporarily lost in the system focus of the moment. In one sense, this is understandable. How can a senior executive reach out and change 100,000 employees? How can a department manager reach out and transform even 10 people? It is hard to conceive of changing individuals, so we naturally reach out and try to pull one or two organizational levers, which we hope in turn will change the individuals. We reach out for the incentive lever or the organizational structure lever. We do this for a good reason. These levers do have an impact on people. Unfortunately, far too often their impact is less than we imagine or hope.

Within the last 50 years, research has consistently demonstrated that to employees, organizational elements such as strategy, structure, or even compensation and incentive systems are abstract and remote. In contrast, the example they see in their boss, the reinforcement they get from their peers, or the punishment they get from customers is much closer—it is *proximate*, in academic speak. Research further demonstrates that proximate factors drive people's behaviors significantly more than distant factors.

This is one reason why transformation levers such as "reorganization" do not produce the results most executives hope for. This disappointment and our inability to see the limitations of new org charts in transforming people are partly why we see reorganization after reorganization. In many firms it looks as if executives never graduated from the childhood game of musical chairs. These executives seem to have forgotten (or perhaps never really understood) that a new org chart has an impact only when individual people on the charts behave differently. If the boxes and reporting lines change, but the attitudes and behaviors remain, so do the results.

But just to make sure that there is no misunderstanding, let us say again that changing strategies, structures, or systems *is* important to transformations. However they enable the transformation; they are not *the* transformation. Unfortunately, in too many cases, executives view these valuable means as the ends. Once the strategy, structure, or system is changed, they think the job is done and that "the rest will naturally happen." Nothing could be further from the truth! The crux of success—or in other words, the key to overcoming the failure to finish—lies in changing a large number of individuals, not in pulling organizational levers.

Unfortunately, changing individuals is not easy, especially if the change required is dramatic. Gravity remains a powerful opponent. Consider that a plane flying across the Atlantic Ocean will burn one-third of its fuel just taking off and getting to cruising altitude. Yet, if at 35,000 feet the pilot determines that the hard part is over and kicks back and pulls the throttle back as well, the plane will come crashing down into the Atlantic and never reach its destination. Changing people is no different. Tremendous energy and effort are required to get people to move. However, the change journey is far from over at that point. There is still a long way left to travel.

As we discussed earlier in the book, people are programmed to survive and as a consequence naturally stick with what has worked, what has proven successful. Most people do not walk by faith. Most people wisely live by the philosophy of *seeing is believing*. If they did not, they would follow any wild, unproven, fanciful idea that came along. In fact, many employees believe that this is what is wrong with senior managers. Employees call it "management by best seller." Too many managers simply grab onto the latest best-selling idea without really knowing whether it will work.

Employees wisely walk in the proven paths of past success and let those well-worn maps guide them. In that wisdom, they rightly resist changes based on whims; they believe in and stick with what they have seen work. The gravity and pull of their previous ways of thinking and behaving exert a constant and compelling force. In contrast, a new destination and path seem to require letting go of gravity, floating in the air, and walking by faith for employees. For most, faith is not an easy concept. As evidence, just ask any clergy, priest, pastor, monk, or rabbi. Trying to get at least some people to change from "seeing is believing" to "believing is seeing" is hard work. A mission statement does not do it. A new organizational chart will not cut it. Faith is not about words or boxes and lines. Faith is about trust.

Employees ask themselves, "Do I trust the promised outcomes? Do I trust my own ability to behave in new ways and achieve the desired results? Do I trust that if I put in all this time and effort to walk this path, the rug will not be yanked out from under me, and a new strategy, structure, and system will be announced just as I'm getting the hang of doing the new right things?"

If you are trying to get employees to think and behave differently, their willingness initially to walk by faith is a function of how much they trust you. If they trust you, they will venture forth and stay on the path. If they don't, they won't.

While this is true, it is beginning to sound a bit philosophical, so let's bring it down to a concrete and practical level. Consider the case of our airline gate agent Sam, working for Your Average Airline (YAA). As the name implies, YAA is not bad but is not particularly good at customer service. However, the new CEO has announced that YAA plans to win the competitive battle by putting the customer first. He even names the new strategy and change program "Customer 1st."

Sam listens to the CEO's presentation about why treating customers badly destroys loyalty and hurts organizational performance. Sam pays careful attention to the arguments about why putting the customer first will differentiate YAA and lead customers to fly YAA more often. He even listens closely enough to see that with more loyal customers and higher occupancy (*load factors* in the CEO's lingo), the company will make more money, and as a consequence Sam will have a more secure and brighter future. Sam begins to accept the new map and destination—the land of Customer 1st. He begins to alter his mental terrain.

YAA's new CEO, being brighter than most, not only presents a clear picture for *why* Customer 1st is a great idea, but also *how* Sam can achieve it. He is provided the required resources. Sam is given training about how to handle customer complaints at the gate and how to speak in a tone that comes across more pleasantly to customers. The path to the land of Customer 1st begins to come into clearer focus. Sam begins to see not only the destination, but also the path that could lead there. Why doesn't Sam at this point just take off running down the path without a moment's reflection in his rearview mirror?

Sam, like all workers, is smart. He does not act on simple blind faith. Instead, he acts on what he believes will give him the best return for his investment. He almost unconsciously makes comparisons between the ratio of effort and reward of the old with the effort and reward of the new.

In the past, it took little effort for Sam to put the customer 2nd, 3rd, or 10th in his priorities. In fact, it was quite easy *not* to be *customer-centric* (one of the other key buzzwords used in the Customer 1st training program Sam attended). Up to this point, Sam has had little trouble being Sam-centric.

For example, recently a customer came running up to the gate, completely out of breath, but still shouting, "I need to get on that plane." The plane was still at the gate, but the final passenger count was completed and the door was about to be closed. Sam was tired and didn't feel like being particularly pleasant. It took little effort to say in a fairly unsympathetic tone, "I'm sorry, boarding is closed." The customer challenged, "What do you mean, closed? I can still see the plane. It's still at the gate. Besides, I'm late because of a stupid mechanical problem on one of your other flights." Without any effort Sam replied, "As I said, boarding is closed." It also didn't take much effort to tune out the passenger's ravings that followed. Sam simply walked away. Sam's effort or investment was low.

What about the benefits—the return on his investment? Surely Sam could *not* have liked the ranting and raving of the irate customer. True, he did not. However, the ranting and raving were not all that negative for Sam, partly because over time, Sam had become quite skilled at tuning them out. What were the positive rewards of being Sam-centric rather than customer-centric? Power and control. The customer did not get on the plane for one simple reason—because Sam said so. In Sam's book that was not a bad outcome at all. In fact, it felt pretty good. When it came to looking for a good effort to outcome ratio, Sam did not have to walk by faith. He knew from experience that "customer last" gave him a good return on his effort. One ounce of effort ("I'm sorry, boarding is closed")—three pounds of reward ("I control your life").

Now consider the same situation, but with the new Customer 1st orientation. Assuming that the customer arrives late enough that it is not within Sam's authority to get him on the plane, Sam still has to turn down the customer. However, the new Customer 1st strategy asks him to put much more effort into both the words and tone he uses. The customer still shouts, "I need to get on that plane!" Sam still has to say, "I'm sorry, but boarding is closed." But this time he also has to work hard to convey a tone of understanding and sympathy. The customer still challenges, "What do you mean, closed? I can still see the plane. It's still at the gate. Besides, I'm late because of a stupid mechanical problem on one of your other flights." Now the new investments required by the new Customer 1st strategy start to pile up. Sam has to think into the customer's situation and convey even greater sympathy. Sam has to think, "I can understand this customer's frustration. Anyone would be frustrated in his shoes."

Still, sympathy alone is not enough. The new Customer 1st organizational transformation requires more. Whereas before, Sam could have just tuned out the customer, now he must put significantly more effort into to solving the customer's problem. To do this well, Sam needs to know what other flights on YAA will get the customer to his destination and what flights on alternative airlines might also work. In the same instant that Sam must process this information, he also needs to say something like, "I can imagine how frustrating the situation is, and I will do whatever I can to help you get to London. We have another flight in 40 minutes that I think I can get you on. I may even be able to upgrade you."

For all his extra investment of attitude and energy, what does Sam get? At first, he is not sure. The first time he tries this new approach, he has to walk by the faith he puts in the trainer's or his boss's promise. Sam is hoping for the smile and "thank you" that had been promised, but what does he get? The first time he tries this new approach he gets a customer who fires back, "I don't care about an upgrade or leaving later, I need to get on *that* plane. What part of *that* plane don't you understand?"

At this point Sam is tempted to retaliate, but instead he exercises even more faith in the new destination and path, so instead says, "I appreciate your frustration, but as I said, I can get you on our next flight to London." Eventually the customer relents and agrees to go on a later flight without so much as a "thank you" before stomping off.

Unconsciously, Sam compares the return on investment ratios (ROI) of the old and the new. The old way: Not much effort and a nice reward of feeling powerful. The new way: Lots of effort and not that much reward. Should Sam continue to have faith that over time the rewards will improve, that customers will smile and thank him? Should he continue to believe that eventually their smiles and "thank you" will translate into better performance for the company and a more secure and rewarding future for him?

Unfortunately, Sam is alone with his thoughts. There was no one else at the gate during the encounter—no boss, no peer. No one was around to say, "Nice job." No one was there to encourage him to have faith and hang in there.

Repeat this one scene over and over again, and it is easy to see why Sam gets tired. If Sam gets tired, it is easy to see how the gravitational pull of Sam's old mental map could overpower the initial momentum of his initial movement toward the new right thing. Multiply Sam by several hundred other similar gate agents, and it is easy to see why the new Customer 1st strategy might get going but then fail to finish.

A way to visualize this is in terms of learning curves. Sam is already well up the learning curve of the old model. He is very proficient at a "customer last" approach. As with any learning curve, high proficiency naturally produces the targeted results, as illustrated in Figure 6.1. Targeted results naturally reinforce the behavior that produced them, and as a consequence, at this point you get a mutually reinforcing cycle.

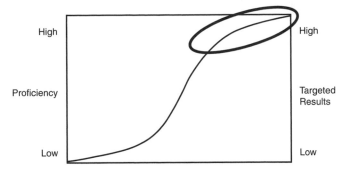

Figure 6.1 High proficiency naturally produces targeted results.

When you go up a *new* learning curve, it is the first part of the curve that is problematic. Whether the learning curve involves learning a language, musical instrument, or Customer First behavior, the first part of any learning curve is characterized by lots of efforts, poor proficiency, and poor results. Fifty years of research in psychology has clearly proven that poor results naturally extinguish the antecedent behavior; psycho-babble for poor results tend to kill the behavior that brought on the poor results, as illustrated in Figure 6.2.

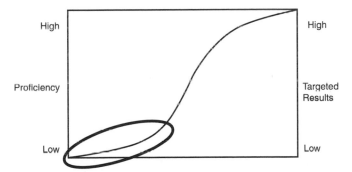

Figure 6.2 Poor proficiency naturally produces poor results.

In sum, change efforts fail to finish because people get tired. They get tired in an absolute sense because change requires energy and effort. The more substantial the change, the more energy and effort must be expended in targeting change in individual employees. More important than the absolute level of energy required is the tiredness that comes from the effort of walking a new path that seems to provide an inferior ROI to an individual employee. Employees get tired of walking by the vapor of faith when the concreteness of the past learning curve they have already mastered waits with open arms to welcome them back (see Figure 6.3). For most people, returning to the fun enjoyed with high proficiency in the past competency is much preferred over the frustration of low proficiency with the new competency.

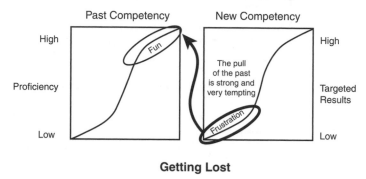

Figure 6.3 The pull of past proficiency.

Getting Lost

Because major transformations of people and organizations are long journeys, people not only get tired along the way, but they can also get lost—very lost. Over the long transformational journey, they lose track of where they started, where they are, and where that places them relative to where they thought they wanted to be and go. Once all this uncertainty sets in and without any helpful map of the territory, employees feel lost and pressing ahead is not very compelling.

To understand this, we need only return to Sam, our gate agent. When we last left Sam, he was getting tired. It took lots of extra effort to put customers first. In many cases, that extra effort was not yielding extra benefits. Fortunately for YAA, Sam was willing to walk a bit more by faith than the average person. Sam knows from past experiences that seeing usually is believing, but sometimes believing is seeing. He knows that sometimes you see something only after you believe in it first. He trusts you, his boss, which makes it easier to have faith in the future. Consequently, he persists in his Customer 1st efforts. He gets some encouragement from you, and he pays special attention to peers, who also seem to be trying. Sam tries to ignore those colleagues who have only bad things to say about the whole Customer 1st notion.

Six months go by. Sam has been working on being more sympathetic, using the phrases he was taught, and solving customer problems more efficiently and effectively. He feels as though he has made some progress, but how much? He is not sure. "What about the rest of the organization?" he wonders. "Are they working as hard as I am?" In his immediate work group, Sam knows that he is in the minority. Most of the others are not really taking this Customer 1st thing all that seriously. "Is my work group typical, or are most of the other groups moving down the path? Have any of my efforts made any difference to customers? Have the collective efforts made any difference? Are load factors up? Are customer satisfaction levels up?" Sam just doesn't know where things stand. He is starting to feel lost. In which case, why should he keep moving forward?

As Sam's questions suggest, he is concerned both about his personal position as well as that of the company. He wants to know how far he has come personally. He has a sense that he has made progress, but he is not sure how much distance he has covered and how much more remains. He also wants to know how far the company has come. Sam does not want to be the only one who is putting in all this extra effort. He knows that many of the personal benefits (a more secure future) depend on organizational benefits (better financial performance) and that he alone cannot bring about the desired organizational results. If others are not doing what he is doing, if others have not made the progress he has made, then Sam has no hope of seeing the benefits in which he has believed and trusted.

Unfortunately, no baseline measure was ever taken of customer satisfaction with Sam's pre-Customer 1st initiative behavior. Neither Sam nor his boss really knows how unhappy or happy customers were with Sam before the new strategy got underway. Perhaps more unfortunately still is that no measure has been taken since. Sam feels like fewer customers stomp away unhappy and more customers smile and say "thank you," but the changes have been so small over so many days that the difference is hard to see and remember vividly.

At the corporate level of YAA, though, there were some baseline measures. For example, corporate had measures of complaints per thousand customers before the transformation. In fact, ranking as one of the worst airlines on this measure was one of the key drivers for the Customer 1st transformation. Company executives have tracked customer complaints per thousand over the last several months. They also have been able to track the level of repeat business from frequent fliers as one important measure of customer satisfaction. Finally, senior management even had an outside consulting firm conduct some customer satisfaction surveys early in the program, as well as more recently.

Not surprisingly, the results were mixed. YAA was making progress. The number of complaints per thousand was down significantly. YAA had moved from last to 5th best on this measure. However, customer satisfaction was actually down. The consultants explained that this was largely a function of raised expectations. Before the transformation, YAA customers had little reason to expect good treatment. With the launch of Customer 1st and the resulting media attention, customers' expectations went up. Although Customer 1st behaviors improved, they did not improve as fast as expectations, and as a consequence, customer satisfaction scores actually dropped.

Executives of YAA worried that disseminating this and other information presented too many risks. What if competitors acquired this privileged information? What if employees got disheartened by the drop in customer scores and were too unsophisticated to appreciate the explanation? What if someone leaked this information to the media? These and a hundred other questions like them kept YAA's executives from letting anyone know how things were actually going.

As Sam's boss, you've heard rumors about how things are going, but no one has shared any concrete numbers with you. When Sam asks about progress, you can only say that you have not heard anything official. When Sam asks about his personal progress, what do you say? You tried telling him that he is doing fine, but he did not seem satisfied and wanted to know what specifically was going well and what he should work on. Your comment "just keep up the good work" did *not* put a smile on Sam's face.

Is it little wonder that Sam is not only a bit tired, but is feeling lost as well? If this were a physical trek through the wilderness, how long would we expect Sam to keep going if he was unsure of where he was, the progress he had made, or how much farther it was to where he wanted to go?

Even after getting to see that the old right thing is now wrong and recognizing what the new right thing is, and even getting employees to believe in the path that will take them from doing the new right thing poorly to doing it well, it is easier to understand why change efforts often falter. They falter because people get tired and lost and therefore fail to finish. They do not go far or fast enough. Those at the controls fail to apply the right power and thrust after takeoff, and the third gravitational force pulls the flight of fancy crashing back to earth.

Overcoming the Final Brain Barrier

Chapter 7, "Solutions and Tools for Breaking through Barrier #3: Helping People Fight through the Finish," outlines the keys to overcoming this third and final brain barrier and force of gravity. Without this knowledge—even though a change project has broken through the barriers of seeing and believing—there is little hope of achieving a lasting change.

Once Chapter 7 has laid out these key steps, Chapter 8, "Pulling It All Together," walks back through the principles and applies them in a set of integrated examples. With the model firmly in place and integrated with the challenge of growth, Chapter 9, "Getting Ahead of the Change Curve," takes the final pragmatic step to ensure the effective application in real life.

7

Solutions and Tools for Breaking through Barrier #3: Helping People Fight through the Finish

Given all the time and energy it takes to overcome the first two brain barriers and get people to see and move, it is sometimes heartbreaking to watch all that success go down in flames because of a failure to finish. As we explained in the last chapter, failure to finish is primarily a function of people getting tired or getting lost. These two culprits keep people from moving fast or far enough to achieve and sustain success. The antidotes to getting tired and getting lost are champions and charting.

Providing Champions

Remember how tired Sam, our gate agent with YAA, got even after he saw and believed in the Customer 1st change? He planted the seed of Customer 1st in his behavior, but like all seeds, it did not sprout immediately or grow into full bloom overnight. It needed consistent care and nurturing. Like a seed, it needed the most attention when it was young. Sam's first few experiments at the new Customer 1st behavior were the most critical. That is when the seed is the most vulnerable. Deny it a bit of water just after it is planted, and it has a good chance of dying.

YAA was lucky to get Sam to try the experiment, given that the rewards were by no means certain. Where was the champion to help nurture, water, and feed this new seed? It would be just plain unrealistic to expect Sam or anyone else to play champion to themselves. Without a champion of the change, Sam will tire, slow down his attempts to change, and likely quit far short of the final destination.

However, when most people talk about change champions, they talk about ensuring leadership support for the change in high, powerful places. While high and mighty champions are necessary to get a strategic change past Barrier #1, they deliver virtually no impact on breaking through Barrier #3. How can this be?

To understand this, just for a moment put yourself in Sam's position. You see the need to change, have made the move, and even started to behave differently. However, because you are in the early part of the learning or change curve, you are not yet proficient at the new behaviors. Your low proficiency naturally produces less-than-desired results. So when you tried to exhibit Customer 1st behavior, showed empathy, and tried to solve the customer's problem and the customer still yelled and cursed at you, at that moment, how much do you care that the CEO is 100 percent in support of the Customer 1st strategic change? At that moment, you don't care if the CEO, chairman, and all the king's men are tried-and-true blue 1,000 percent in support of Customer 1st. At that moment in time, the only champion who can make any difference and increase the odds that you don't get tired, give up, and fail to finish is the champion who comes up next to you and says, "Sam, look, I know that didn't go very well, but that was a good effort. You tried to show empathy and solve the customer's problem. Hang in there." To be crystal clear, when it comes to Barrier #3, it is change champions standing next to the action, not sitting upstairs in some lofty tower, that make the difference between failing or fighting through to the finish.

For a large-scale change effort, it may not be practical or possible to put in place the required number of champions (let alone quality) to ensure that all the early walks of faith are supported and reinforced, that all the early seeds that are planted stay fed and watered. In these cases, it is critical to identify and designate some early *launch* sites. They should be called "launch sites," not pilots or test cases, or anything else that can leave people questioning executive commitment to the change. Early launch sites should be staffed with trained and motivated champions right next to the action as it happens. Only in this way can you have a chance to break the hold of the third gravitational force behind the third barrier of change; and only then do you have a reasonable hope of helping employees avoid getting tired, slowing down, and giving up too early.

Champions must know what to look for and what to reinforce. They must know how to reinforce what they're looking for. Imagine again being Sam's boss. What is it you are looking for? Are you looking for results or efforts? Lots of change books talk about "celebrating early wins." That places an emphasis on results. The problem is that early in the change curve, proficiency is low and so great results to celebrate are sparse. As a consequence, in our experience, the intent of the notion "celebrate early wins" is right on but the focus is dead wrong. Initially, you are looking for efforts, not results. Early on you will see lots of good efforts to celebrate and not so many early wins.

At first, Sam is not going to be good at Customer 1st, scientists at QuadQ are not going to be good at working in cross-functional teams, and sales people at Xerox are not going to be good at document solutions. The natural consequences that follow initially less-than-stellar capabilities on average will be negative. We don't need 60 years of research (though it's there) to tell us that if left uncompensated, natural and negative consequences will kill the desired, new behavior. The job of change champions is to counteract this natural force. In sum, to do this you must:

- Be close to the action.
- Look for desired efforts, not results.
- Counteract natural negative consequences with positive ones.

The determination of the right positive rewards for desired efforts takes us right back to Chapter 5, "Solutions and Tools for Breaking through Barrier #2: Helping People Make the Move." There is no substitute for knowing your people and understanding what types of rewards they value. For some it is simple praise, for others it is highlighting that they are doing better than other employees. Indeed, there is no magic formula for determining which types of rewards you should use to encourage early change efforts. All we can offer is a framework of rewards from which you can be reasonably sure there are one or two that fit virtually any subordinate you have. Only you can discover or know which one or two are the most powerful for a given individual.

This is why change champions are needed exactly where the rubber meets the road. Champions reinforce desired behaviors even when the targeted efforts do not generate desired results—at first. To ensure champions are in place to compensate for this initial gravitational pull, we provide two straightforward tools.

The first helps you make explicit three key elements of championing. First, it is absolutely critical to identify in advance the "rubber-meets-the-road" behaviors for the strategic change. What must be different for the change to gain traction and produce an impact? (Surprisingly, only 5 percent of a tire touches the road at any point in time, but that 5 percent of rubber meeting the road delivers all the traction required to keep moving forward.) Second, it is helpful to identify in advance likely negative consequences for less-than-ideal proficiency in following the new map. Champions must compensate for these outcomes by reinforcing the desired behaviors so that employees do not get too discouraged and fail to finish. Finally, it is important to make explicit what actions change champions should take when people exhibit the right behaviors, but do not produce the desired consequences. We use the following tool (shown in Table 7.1) to help change champions map out these three key elements.

Table 7.1 Tool for Mapping Out Champion Actions

Rubber-Meets-the-Road Behaviors	Likely Negative Consequences of Initial Poor Proficiency	Key Champion Compensatory Actions
1.	1. 2.	1. 2.
2.	1. 2.	1. 2.
3.	1. 2.	1. 2.
4.	1. 2.	1. 2.
5.	1. 2.	1. 2.
6.	1. 2.	1. 2.

Stopping here, however, assumes that champions are capable of providing the needed compensatory actions. This is not usually the case. For most front-line change champions, the role likely requires new behaviors. Therefore, simply but systematically assessing required capabilities, current capabilities, resulting gaps, and needed bridging actions are a must. Table 7.2 illustrates the tool we use to accomplish this.

Table 7.2   **Tool for Mapping Out Champion Capabilities**

Champion Assessment			
Required Capability	Current Capability	Gap	Bridging Actions
		YES NO	1. 2.
		YES NO	1. 2.
		YES NO	1. 2.
		YES NO	1. 2.
		YES NO	1. 2.
		YES NO	1. 2.

By using these two tools, you will gain a clear understanding of where and why people will likely get tired, and you will have the champions and actions in place to compensate for sluggish behaviors. These tools will help you maintain change momentum until improvements in proficiency can produce positive consequences that naturally reinforce desired behaviors.

Charting Progress

Making sure that Sam has a champion (by the way, the person does not have to be Sam's boss) by his side when he plants his first few Customer 1st seeds is necessary, but not sufficient. You will recall that after several weeks and months, Sam began to wonder how he was doing and how much progress the organization was making. Without this knowledge, he started to feel lost; by feeling lost, he had little incentive to keep going.

When it comes to measuring progress, it needs to be done both at the executive suite and in the trenches. All the Sams of YAA need to know how the organization is doing. Part of their reward is tied to the organization's performance. That performance—the good, bad, and ugly—needs to be communicated. Without it, Sam is left to imagine the worst. If he imagines that progress is not being made, why should he keep going? In our experience—in 99 cases out of 100—the actual performance of the change effort, no matter how bad, is not as bad as people can imagine if left to their own devices. In the absence of information from on high, employees will still imagine something 100 percent of the time. This point is critical and worth repeating. People cannot and do not suspend judgment and conclusions for long. *Lacking any information or conclusions from management, employees will form their own.* Normally, they assume that if things were good, they would hear about it. Therefore, if they are not hearing anything, then things must be bad—really bad. The key point here is that anyone who believes that employees will over-interpret bad news and hopes that if no news is given to employees that they will simply suspend conclusions is utterly mistaken and misguided.

Also, the worry that Sam and others are not smart or sophisticated enough to understand such complicated issues as to why customer satisfaction went down even as Customer 1st behaviors increased is also misguided. If Sam is smart and sophisticated enough to understand why Customer 1st was the new right way, how did he suddenly turn dumb? If he can grasp the path forward, he can understand the potential sidetracks.

In addition to organization-level measurement and communication of progress, achieving success also requires monitoring and communicating at the individual level. Sure, Sam is concerned about how the organization is doing, but likely even more concerned about his own progress. Either his boss needs a reliable intuitive means of measuring progress, or he needs to follow a structured and formal one. In either case, Sam needs to know how much progress he has made. He needs to know if that level of progress fails to meet, adequately meets, or exceeds expectations. He needs to know how much farther there is to go. He needs advice, counsel, and help on how to make further improvements. Without "micro"-level monitoring and feedback, all the "macro"-level details in the world about the organization's progress may not keep Sam from getting lost, giving up, and failing to finish.

Change Performance Dashboard

Except for the simplest of change initiatives, there are typically dozens of measures of progress that we might look at, creating hundreds of messages to then communicate to people. To solve this challenge, we take a page from flying and driving. Although confronted with potentially hundreds of cues, effective pilots and drivers alike focus on a few key instruments. Consequently, these instruments are usually best seen in a "heads-up" display on a plane (or a dashboard on a car). In airplanes, speed, altitude, and heading are key measures. Likewise, any change initiative must include a *limited* number of key measures to keep your eye on. You might call this your "heads-up" display for change measurement (see Figure 7.1).

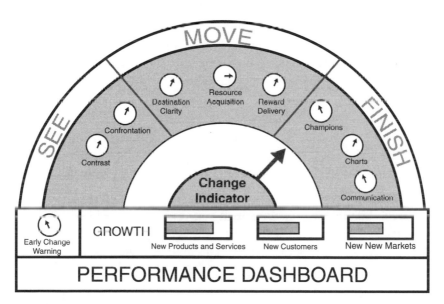

Figure 7.1   Change performance dashboard.

From our experience, five preparation elements belong on the dashboard. While none are new, they are critical for breaking through the failure to finish change barrier and their neglect is often a key reason so many change initiatives that get moving don't last.

- **What**. First, identify what you believe the key measures are. For example, if we return to our gate agent Sam, customer complaints are clearly an important measure of whether the Customer First initiative is working. Customer satisfaction may also be an important measure.

- **How**. Next, you have to determine how the measure will be assessed. For example, an airline might measure complaints based on the number of written complaints received per 1,000 passengers. Customer satisfaction might be measured via a survey given to a random set of customers.

- **When**. Third, it's critical to establish how often the measures will be taken. For example, some measures are more difficult and costly to procure than others, while other outcomes take longer to formulate, and therefore measures are useful only if taken with longer time intervals between assessments.

- **Baseline**. Once measures and methods are determined, establishing a baseline of performance is critical before the change initiative gets underway. Without a baseline, it is difficult to know how much progress has been made.

- **Target**. Finally, establishing target performance levels is also critical. Should Sam be shooting for less than 10 complaints per month, or less than 1? The tool in Table 7.3 can help you capture these change measurement issues.

Table 7.3 Tool for Mapping Out Progress

Measure	Method	Interval	Base Line	Target
1.				
2.				
3.				
4.				
5.				

When it comes to charting progress on these measures, there are as many approaches as there are companies. As far as we know, no research says definitively that one method of charting progress trumps another. What we can say from our experience is the following:

- First, graphs have a stronger impact on people than the mere numbers behind them.

- Second, charts that show progress over time relative to the final destination help the most to avoid people feeling lost.

Figure 7.2 illustrates sample chart that captures these two points.

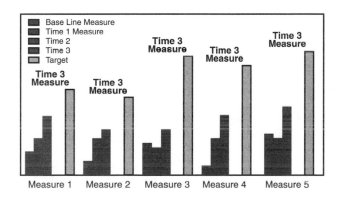

Figure 7.2   **Chart of change progress.**

Change Communication Plan

With the key elements of measures established, your next step is determining the general communication plan. Whole books are devoted to effective communication plans, so we won't try to reproduce all those ideas here. Rather, we will stick to the fundamentals that everyone knows, but are useful to review.

- **Who.** Any communication plan starts by determining "who" the information receiver will be. In our experience, companies tend to err in the direction of sharing change progress with too few people. Whenever we assess employees' satisfaction with communication, especially related to strategic change initiatives, we have never found a situation where employees felt that too many people were informed as to how things were progressing. In almost every case, employees who were excluded from the communication believed that they should have been included. Now, we are not suggesting that these employees were always right and should have been included, but their feelings do illustrate how much easier it is to err on the side of limiting the "who" of communication plans too much than in expanding the recipient list too far.

- **What**. Next, the communication plan should determine "what" will be shared. As mentioned earlier, it's best to share the good, the bad, and even the ugly. To think that certain people can help you bring about a needed change, and to also believe that they are not mature enough to understand how the change is really going, communicates a double standard loud and clear.

- **When**. "When" is the third element to determine in a communication plan. We should take some measures more often than others. Consequently, in some cases not everything is communicated at the same time. In general, it's a mistake to wait until everything is known before communicating anything. People can easily feel lost while waiting for perfect information; therefore, some information sooner is better than all the information later.

- **How**. Finally, in this age of various communication mediums, deciding on "how" to communicate progress presents unique challenges. Due to the range of options (email, voice mail, snail mail, video, face-to-face, presentations, and so on), you may need to choose a different medium for different times or different content. For example, content such as declining customer satisfaction scores after the launch of a Customer 1st program is probably best communicated through more complex and rich mediums such as live presentations or videos versus mass emails. Table 7.4 provides a tool that can help you map out the basics of your change communication plan.

Table 7.4   Tool for Mapping Out Communication Plan

Communication Plan			
Who	What	When	How

Again, this book's purpose is not to outline all the details and nuances to designing a communication plan, but simply to reinforce that a plan is necessary and that you should incorporate four core elements into it.

Pulling It All Together

Taken together, the model we have worked through maps directly on to our framework for outlining the barriers to remapping change. Consequently, if you can remember the barriers seeing, moving, and finishing, you can remember the model for effectively remapping change. It is as simple as the 1, 2, 3: See, Move, Finish.

These three stages in implementing change successfully are designed to correspond with and overcome the three barriers of change.

Failure to See is a function of entrenched, successful maps. The more successful they are, the more blinding they are. To break through the first barrier, people must see that the environment has changed and the old right thing is now wrong. They must see (literally a mental image of) the new right thing. It takes high contrast and confrontation to break through and help employees see that the old right way is now wrong and to see the new vision. Heightening contrast and confrontation requires focusing on the core differences, juxtaposing their descriptions, repeating the message, and putting people in inescapable experiences to force the contrast.

Failure to Move occurs because people are not motivated to go from doing the wrong thing well to doing the right thing poorly. To break through the second brain barrier, people must move along the path that will take them from doing the new right thing poorly to doing it well. It takes ensuring that the target is clear, that the capabilities and tools are in place, and that rewards are provided in order for employees to believe that they can go from doing the right thing poorly to doing it well.

Finally, *Failure to Finish* happens because employees get tired and lost, and therefore do not go fast or far enough. Achieving success requires champions in place to reinforce and encourage employees the first few times the seeds of the change are planted, and to applaud the first few steps in their walk of faith. It requires monitoring progress and communicating individual and collective improvement.

In combination, See, Move, and Finish are the keys to overcoming the powerful and persistent forces of gravity that can hold back lasting change.

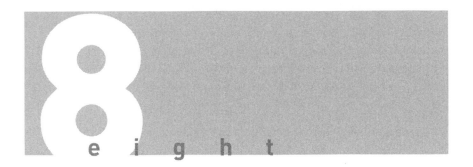

Pulling It All Together

So far we have broken down and covered the elements of our change model separately. Although this helps highlight and clarify the specific parts and steps, leading change in real situations requires pulling all three elements together in an integrated fashion. The purpose of this chapter is to help you do just that. However, because leading strategic change is not confined to CEOs, we want to start the integration process with a look at a middle manager's experience leading a strategic change. Also, because leading effective change can often require leading it, not just with internal employees, but also with external customers and suppliers, we examine an example of this as well. Finally, because for many of us leading strategic change requires not just changing others, but changing ourselves as well, we end this chapter with a look at a personal journey of change that one CEO took in order to bring about strategic change in his company. Our hope is that by walking through a few diverse examples, you will have a reasonably good sense of how the three core elements of our change framework come together in concrete and practical ways.

One Call That's All

Our first example takes place where the majority of changes, in fact, need to happen—the middle of organizations. We start with this example not only because it is where the majority of strategic changes actually happen, but also because leading change at this level often requires not just getting people below and around you to change, but getting people *above* you (bosses and bosses of bosses) to change as well. As every reader knows from experience, leading strategic change upward is arguably one of the most difficult tasks.

The example we want to examine involves a senior middle manager trying to lead a change in a company that enjoyed a long history of success—a history of doing the right thing and doing it very well. However, a key technology has emerged to create a new opportunity to better serve existing customers. In this situation, the top executives are already sold on the general utility of the new technology and have approved its adoption. However, they have not appreciated the concrete implications of adopting the technology for the real operating parts of the organization. The reality of the situation is that until top executives appreciate this, employing the new technology could actually *hurt* customer satisfaction and sales, not help them.

The company is Federal Express (FedEx), and the manager facing the change challenge is Laurie Tucker. No doubt all readers know of the phenomenal growth and success FedEx experienced from its founding in 1971, when on April 17 it shipped 186 packages to 25 cities. Its original operating model is now legendary. Fred Smith had the idea that if you established a central hub connected by spokes out to key cities, you could literally ship packages from one place to another overnight. He believed that customers were increasingly valuing speed and, as a consequence, would pay for the overnight delivery of certain packages and documents.

This fundamental business model worked brilliantly throughout the 1970s and into the 1980s. In the mid-1980s, software technology and computing power increased to the point that it became possible and cost-effective for FedEx to tag and track every one of the millions of packages it transported per day all along their journey from shipping origin to shipping destination. With this technology, FedEx was able to offer customers the ability to call FedEx and find out where their packages were at any point in the process. FedEx discovered that customers loved this ability because it gave them peace of mind while packages were in transit and secure confirmation when packages were delivered. To support this service, call centers were set up so that customers could inquire about the status of their packages. As a result of this service's popularity, in short order FedEx had 16 call centers just within the U.S.

By 1998, FedEx saw an additional technology—the Internet—providing a new means of enhancing the tracking element of FedEx's customer value proposition. With the Internet, customers would not need to dial into a call center to obtain an update on the status of their package, but could simply go on the web. Using the unique tracking number assigned to their package, customers could look up its status and time (day or night) from the office, on the road, or at home, without waiting on the phone if the call center was busy. As expected, most customers loved this enhanced aspect of FedEx's tracking service. The new Internet-based tracking system would also help FedEx reduce costs by lowering the number of new call-center representatives it had to hire. The lower costs would, in turn, help grow earnings. Senior executives made the strategic decision to launch the new service and by 1999, the company had established a website that customers could log into and track their packages.

Both anticipated and unanticipated consequences came from this strategic initiative. First, as expected, FedEx experienced some revenue growth as customers voted with their wallets in favor of this new service. Customers did in fact like the ability to check on the status of their packages any time they wanted with just a click. This was especially true of packages being sent internationally. As hoped, repeat business increased; however, not all customers were happy. Unexpectedly, as some customers tracked their packages, they then called in with more sophisticated questions about their package's movement in general, along with questions about the website and how to use it in particular. The problem was that call center reps had no access to the website and were trained in narrow specialties to answer very specific questions. Unable to answer questions about the website or questions outside their area of specialization, call reps would pass customers along in a series of call transfers to try and get the various questions answered. Not surprisingly, this often resulted in delays as the customer waited for the next transfer and too often in dropped calls during one or another of the transfers. Neither result delighted customers. Rather, both infuriated them. As a consequence, the new technology for these customers actually lowered their satisfaction and level of repeat business, and increased the negative word-of-mouth they put on the street about FedEx.

The challenge of changing the old mental map to a new one regarding how to organize and run a call center fell to Laurie Tucker. Her first task was to change the mental maps of senior managers above her. She needed to help them see that with the advent of the Internet, the old call-center approach of specialized reps, which had worked so well in the past, was not the right approach for the future. She needed to help them see that having reps with higher and broader capabilities and the ability to access all the information a customer might have was the new right thing. The shorthand label for this vision, this "new right thing," was *OneCall*.

Breaking through this first barrier of change was not a simple one, but it was critical. Until the senior executives saw the need for change, Tucker would not be able to get the funds required to make OneCall a reality. In order to create a bit of contrast and confrontation and change senior managers' mental maps, Tucker and her staff created a short video for the board. It showed a customer calling in while looking at the website, posing a number of questions to a frantic and confused call center rep who could only apologize for not being able to help because he could not see the website and was not trained in the areas related to the customer's inquiries. Insult was added to injury for the customer when he was passed from this initial bumbling call rep to another rep, who had to put the customer on hold while he sought out a supervisor, who then inadvertently dropped the call when he came on the line.

The stunning contrast hit the senior executives right between the eyes; they could see and hear in a rich way the failings of the old approach. When contrasted with images of OneCall in which a customer was able in one call to get the desired information and *not* be passed along in a series of frustrating transfers, approval of OneCall was quickly granted.

Because call center employees were directly experiencing the frustrations that came with the old approach, they were more than ready for the change and the new approach. In this sense, call center reps already saw the need for change and were ready for the next part of the change model—making the move.

However, just because employees saw the need for change did not mean that they would instantly change. Without the required capabilities, knowledge, resources, and training, they could anticipate that they would do the new right thing (try to answer all the customer's questions in one call) and do it poorly. As we discussed earlier, this primary problem keeps people from breaking through the Failure to Move barrier even after they see the need for change.

Indeed, in FedEx's case, call reps were somewhat anxious about their ability to fulfill the OneCall vision. Reps knew they had specialized knowledge and wondered how they could possibly know enough to answer all the questions a customer might ask. In fact, it was the depth of their specialized knowledge and their experience answering customers' specialized questions that made them worry if they could ever become knowledgeable enough to answer difficult questions, not just about one area of specialization, but across most areas of specialization. For the OneCall vision to work, call reps would have to be cross-trained in various areas such as customs clearance, hazardous materials restrictions, and the like so that customers did not get passed along in a frustrating series of handoffs. As much "business sense" as OneCall made, not one call rep was interested in going from being competent in their area of specialization to being incompetent across a wide variety of areas. Unless and until reps could see how they could go from being competent in one area of specialization to being competent across a wide variety of areas, they might see the strategic need to change to OneCall but remain unwilling to move in that direction.

On top of this serious concern, most reps had little to no experience with the Internet in general and with the company's website in particular. Therefore, to make the move, not only would reps need web access, but they would also need training on how to use the company's website and how to walk people through the site and its various functions.

Basically, even though Tucker and her team needed to do virtually nothing to help reps see the need to make the change, getting the reps to actually make the move was a serious and complicated undertaking. As we have stressed throughout the book, while breaking through the first barrier and helping people see the need for change is a necessary step in the process, it is an insufficient one.

To break through Barrier #2, Tucker and her team made sure that all the necessary resources were provided so call reps could make the move. The first thing her team did to ensure reps made the move was provide them with access to the company's website and training on how to use it.

Ensuring that reps had the knowledge and ability to answer most customers' questions was a more complicated move. First, Tucker and her team determined that trying to train all reps in everything all at once was a bad idea—it was overwhelming and inefficient. Rather, the team determined that they needed to find out which questions across all areas of specialization were the most common. The team used interviews and other data to determine this. Figuring out the 20 percent of questions that accounted for 80 percent of what customers asked would allow Tucker and her team to get the reps more quickly up this new learning curve than trying to tackle 100 percent of what customers might ask. Using the 20/80 "par ado principle" made it much easier to convince the reps that they could in fact become competent at the new right thing. Once the 20/80 principle was put in place and reps could answer the most common questions across all areas, they were later trained to answer the less common customer questions across various specializations.

Once call reps had the web access and training to deliver the OneCall vision, the next challenge was getting reps to believe they would be rewarded for walking the new path. With the old map, call reps were used to being measured and rewarded on call-time objectives. In other words, the more calls you handled in a day and, therefore, the shorter you made each call, the better. Unfortunately, this contradicted the vision of OneCall. The objective of OneCall was a satisfied customer whose questions were all answered with *one* call to *one* rep. As a consequence, the old call-time measures and rewards had to be dropped. Going forward, reps would be rewarded with bonuses based on customer satisfaction and augmented by other criteria, including efficiency, accuracy, and friendliness.

To ensure that the change did not get stuck at the third barrier and Fail to Finish, Tucker and her team did two critical things. First, her team not only measured the results regarding customer satisfaction, efficiency, accuracy, and friendliness, but they also communicated these results back to call centers overall and to reps individually. In addition, supervisors were directed to spend more time listening to call rep conversations so that they could praise reps when they solved thorny, time-consuming customer inquiries and could continue to coach reps and champion the change.

As the destination was made clear, the resources put in place, and a mixture of valued rewards presented to reps, they began to believe in and walk the new OneCall path. The results of achieving this level of belief and follow-through were significant. In fact, at one of the early centers to undergo the transformation, OneCall generated $10 million in additional sales from delighted customers within a few short months after implementation. With 16 total call centers in the U.S. alone, similar results at each center made important contributions to overall customer satisfaction and to company performance.

No doubt as a manager you appreciate that any real-world example such as this is more involved and complicated than can be rendered in a book. Still, hopefully you can see the power of focusing on the three elements of the change model. To help this focus, Table 8.1 summarizes the three elements of the change model and key steps Tucker took in breaking though each barrier and bringing about ultimate success.

Table 8.1 Breakthrough Change at FedEx

Change Step	Actions
See the Need	Created a video to show a clear and compelling contrast between the old and new approaches.
Make the Move	Provided access to the website. Trained reps in navigating the website. Trained reps across many areas of potential questions.
Fight to the Finish	Changed performance criteria from call efficiency to call effectiveness. Charged supervisors with being champions and spending time listening to and coaching reps to ensure follow-through on the change.
Results	Captured cost savings from leveraging technology and employee productivity. Generated significant new revenues in repeat business from satisfied existing customers. Generated new revenues from new customers due to positive word-of-mouth from existing customers.

Growth for a Change

Most firms we have worked with or studied report that growth is one of their more challenging changes. Often one of the greatest obstacles to greater future growth is getting employees (including senior executives) to let go of growth drivers from the past. As we discussed at this book's outset, people are often blind to new opportunities, not because they can't see, but because their eyes are full of what they have seen work so well in the past. When it comes to growth, in many, many cases the firm's *current* low growth was preceded by higher *past* growth. The longer and more dramatic the previous period of growth, the more established employees' mental maps are of what drives growth. The key for new growth in the future is often breaking out of these restrictive mental maps of the past.

This was essentially the case for The Kellogg Company, which we discussed earlier. Almost from the invention of the corn flake, the company's growth, especially through the 1950s, 60s, 70s and even most of the 80s, was driven by cold breakfast cereal sales in the U.S. Arguably, breakfast cereal and the U.S. became the centers of the company's universe. When growth slowed as the demographics and the frantic lifestyles of families in the U.S. changed, along with their morning eating habits, executives at Kellogg were slow to see the need for strategic change in the company.

In situations such as this, we have found that for people to see new avenues of growth you must contrast their limited maps of past drivers with expansive ones of the future. To do this, we use a simple tool that works well across different industries and products.

First, to create a contrast you must make the past growth maps clear and explicit. Relative to growth, we simply ask those we are working with—whether they are senior executives or factory workers—to talk about the existing products and existing customers. We then place their basic descriptions of the products and customers in a box like that illustrated in Figure 8.1. In the mid-1990s, most of Kellogg's revenues were due to cold cereal sales in the U.S.

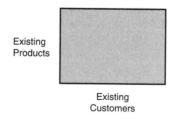

Existing
Products

Existing
Customers

Figure 8.1 **Past growth.**

We then place this box in a larger, two-dimensional matrix, illustrated in Figure 8.2.

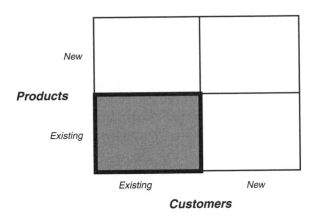

Figure 8.2 Past growth and future opportunities.

As mentioned, for nearly 27 years, breakfast cereal sales in the U.S. dominated the conceptual space for Kellogg's executives. This is why the "existing-existing" box accounted for nearly 80 percent of Kellogg's revenue. Thus, in reality, although Figure 8.2 shows each cell in the matrix of equal size, the reality of the mental map at Kellogg was closer to what is illustrated in Figure 8.3, in which cereal sales in the U.S. account for most of what executives saw.

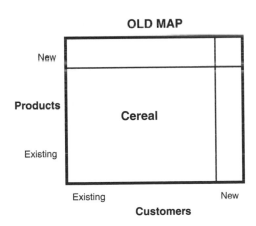

Figure 8.3 "Proportionalizing" past and future growth.

Ironically, as long as the map is viewed as illustrated in Figure 8.3, it will likely remain viewed this way. In other words, if the proportional size of the growth area for new products for existing customers, or existing products for new customers, or new products for new customers is proportionally so small, why should these opportunities be pursued?

They seem so small. As long as they seem small, they will not be pursued, and as long as they are not pursued, they will continue to seem small.

In this situation, how can you help people see the need for change? The old map had worked well for decades. While not always a necessity, sometimes a new perspective requires a new pair of eyes. In Kellogg's case, a new CEO, Carlos Gutierrez, in fact brought a new pair of eyes and a different perspective. Based on his own personal experience, he knew that there was more to the breakfast table globally than what people in Battlecreek, Michigan ate.

The first step in breaking through the first change barrier is to make a compelling contrast between what had been and what could be. The old map in Kellogg was limiting future growth. To help people break out of the limitations of the old growth map, our experience is that you have to make explicit what lies in the "existing-existing" cell of the growth matrix. The next step is to describe and discuss all the possibilities in the other three cells outside the "existing-existing" quadrant. At this point, we then try to gauge the general scale of the new growth opportunities and redraw the matrix to approximate these potential proportions, as illustrated in Figure 8.4 for Kellogg.

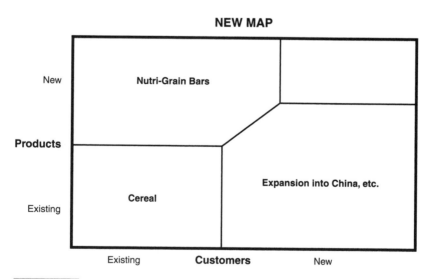

Figure 8.4 Resized growth map.

Even a simple contrast between the old and the new, as illustrated by contrasting Figures 8.3 and 8.4, can often help people recognize the limitations and even distortions of the old map. To be clear, it is not necessary for the new "proportionalized" map to be completely accurate. That is not the point. The purpose is simply to help people see the contrast between what has been and what might be and to recognize that if they don't change their perspective, strategic change for the company is also unlikely!

As helpful as this contrast might be, it is primarily an intellectual one. Because it lacks much of anything experiential, it risks being a "change parade" and capturing people's attention only for a moment, leaving them to go back to what they were doing and thinking before the parade. How might you increase the impact by making the contrast more experiential?

Imagine that, in a meeting with the top executives rather than just drawing the two matrixes illustrated in Figures 8.3 and 8.4, you present to your executive team a large map of the world laid out on the boardroom table. Further imagine that you place on top of various countries of the world map samples of what people in that country typically eat for breakfast. For example, on top of Japan you placed some freshly broiled fish, steaming rice, and miso soup. On top of India, you placed some aromatic Khichri (a mixture of rice, lentils, and spices) and so on. Further imagine that the size of the country on the world map and the size of the portions of breakfast samples are in proportion to the size of the population and breakfast food consumed.

The contrast becomes very clear. Whereas Kellogg had viewed cold breakfast cereal in North America as constituting the heart of growth in the past, it could not be in the future. By placing samples of breakfast dishes from around the world on a proportionally-sized map of the world, executives would literally be able to see, smell, touch, and taste the contrast between where growth came from in the past and where it will reside in the future.

However, you don't have to go global to grow. Even for existing customers in the U.S., they do *not* only eat cereal for breakfast. Thus, while Kellogg's share of the breakfast cereal market in the U.S. had been an impressive 30–35 percent, its share of the overall breakfast food table in the U.S. was significantly lower. At the time, Kellogg had virtually no presence in key food categories such as frozen breakfast foods or yogurts. You don't need to go to India to grow, but you do need to break out of just selling breakfast cereal in Indiana.

Once this contrast was shown to senior executives, making the move required resources. One of the most significant was an investment in a new state-of-the-art center for food and nutrition research to spur new product ideas. New leadership, in particular Donna Banks who became the new senior vice president of worldwide product innovation and operations, put time and attention on new product innovation. As a consequence, subsequent new products were launched at a rate three times greater than in the previous quarter century. Resources were also put into expanding the map beyond the traditional cereal market. For example, in 2001, Kellogg spent $4.56 billion on the acquisition of Keebler Foods, famous for its cookies and crackers, not cereal.

In just five years under the direction of Gutierrez, Kellogg transformed its strategic map for growth. While it continued to grow the "existing-existing" core of the company, the change in its strategic growth map led it into new products with the acquisition of Keebler and new customers through continued geographic expansion. By the time Gutierrez left Kellogg to become the U.S. secretary of commerce in 2004, less than half the company's sales were coming from cereal in the U.S., with nearly a quarter coming from non-cereal sales in this core market. In addition, because of Gutierrez's efforts to push Kellogg deeper into globalization, by the time he left the company Kellogg was operating in 180 countries and generating more than one-third of sales outside the U.S.

The effect of all this was that Kellogg did achieve growth for a change. Whereas in the years just previous to Gutierrez's promotion to CEO, Kellogg's sales and profit growth were in the low single digits; in the five years after, they doubled. Shareholders were rewarded for this change as they saw the value of their shares beat Kellogg's biggest rival, General Mills, by nearly tenfold from 1999–2004, and total shareholder return nearly doubled during this period!

Changing Customers and Suppliers

As difficult as change is inside the company, often it is even more difficult when it requires changing external parties such as customers and suppliers. Dell Computer provides an interesting example of a company that has made significant changes inside and also outside the company in ways that generated both increases in revenues and cash flow.

The PC business has become so price-competitive that margins have shrunk to 2 percent. Consequently, the only way to grow revenue, and especially earnings, is to push costs down and productivity up. With Compaq, Apple, and IBM averaging 50–90 days of finished goods inventory, Dell set the target for its OptiPlex plant at zero! Yes, zero finished goods inventory. To make good on this objective, the plant has no warehouse. The plant was designed so that finished goods were shipped out of the plant as they came off the assembly line. This was no small task, given that the plant produces, on average, more than 20,000 machines (PCs, servers, storage boxes, and more) *each day*!

Furthermore, while its competitors averaged several weeks of component inventory, Dell set the goal of not two weeks, or two days, but two hours of components. To ensure this lean supply system, each of the several receiving docks for different components is roughly 100 square feet, about the size of a large closet. This is also significant when you consider that the overall plant covers a total of more than 200,000 square feet (more than 23 American football fields).

To put in place the automated assembly equipment and software was a significant task, but it has provided impressive benefits. For example, productivity (units produced per person, per hour) increased 160 percent in just the first year. While Dell will not reveal the specific return on investment figures for this plant, the company noted that in 1994 its average return on technological investments was about 30 percent, while in 2000 (the period after which the OptiPlex plant was put in place) Dell's ROI was 300 percent. Clearly this is impressive. However, without changing the way customers order machines and how suppliers provide components, the automated assembly would grind to a screeching halt. This is the part of the change that is perhaps more interesting and provides a different angle from which we can examine how to overcome the three barriers to change.

For Dell, the change process started with the need to change mindsets and behaviors in customers, specifically regarding how they order from Dell. Without orders, there are no products to assemble—by hand labor or by a "lights out" automated factory. More than 85 percent of all Dell orders come from companies, not consumers. In the past, most of Dell's corporate customers had labor-intensive and slow ordering processes. For example, at Litton, when employees wanted to order a computer, they had to fill out, by hand, a requisition form. If they were not careful in reading the hard-to-understand policy guidelines, they would often order a computer with a configuration that was not "approved" for their level or job position. In this case, back would come the requisition from Litton's purchasing department to be redone, by hand, by the employee. Once the requisition was correctly completed, it would then be sent off to the employee's boss, and often the boss's boss, for approval. When the required approvals were obtained (which could take several days or even weeks—depending on how quickly the boss approved the requisition), the requisition would be sent back to purchasing. Once there, it would be checked again to ensure that the requisition specifications met the guidelines; then a purchase order would be issued. Even when the process ran smoothly and there were no mistakes, it took on average just longer than two weeks before a purchase order (PO) was issued. It then took another four weeks for the PO to be processed and a computer from Dell to finally show up at the company's receiving dock. The total time from when the employee put pen (or more sensibly pencil with its handy eraser) to paper to when the computer arrived at the company's receiving docks was 36–40 working days.

However, the process did not end there. Once the computer arrived, it then went through receiving and was logged into property and given a property ID code. After that, it needed to go to IT where it was loaded with the correct software and configured for the company's network system and the like. However, depending on how busy the IT department was at the time, the computer might be in IT from one to two weeks before it would finally wind its way to the user's desk. Once there, more often than not often the user would discover that something about the computer did not work correctly because it was not configured for the network properly, was missing some special software the user required, or something else. Again, depending on how busy (or motivated) IT was, it might take days or weeks to get everything fixed. As a consequence, from the time the computer arrived at the company until the employee was productively utilizing it, it could easily be an additional 5–21 working days.

Taken altogether, the entire process from the time the employee requested the computer to the time he or she was productively using it could be two to three months! When tracked closely, this process involved 12–15 hours of work and added approximately $720 to the computer's $2,300 base purchase price, or effectively a 30 percent increase!

Dell had to help Litton conceive a better way. Dell's vision had several key components. First, Dell would create a customized catalog for the company. This catalog would consist of products and configurations pre-approved by the company. It would even create pre-approved configurations for different levels in the company or for different job categories. As a consequence, when ordering a computer, an employee could not inadvertently order a computer with features that exceeded the guidelines for person's job or level. Once employees had tapped in their order on the custom web page, a requisition was instantly created and sent electronically to their boss. The boss then had 24 hours to respond, or the request was sent to his or her boss for immediate approval. When approved, a purchase order would be electronically and automatically created and sent to Dell. If the requisition was instantly approved when received by the boss, the entire process from requisition to when Dell started making the computer could be 60 seconds! However, under the new approach, the computer would not only be configured with the correct hardware but all of the correct software would be pre-installed as well. In addition, the computer would automatically be given a property ID code and would be logged automatically into the company's system. As a consequence, the computer would never even go through either the receiving department or the IT department of the company, but would be shipped directly from Dell to the employee's desk. Assuming approval of requisitions within 24 hours of its generation, instead of the total order to delivery taking 36–40 working days, it would now take only three to four days!

As fantastic as this tenfold improvement sounds, it was not easy to get customers to change their mindset or behaviors. Dell had to break through and help customers see the need for change. To break through, you must create the contrast between the old and new approach. While there are many different ways to accomplish this, imagine creating a simple but entertaining animated cartoon. Through the cartoon, you see and hear characters walking through the old processes. An employee's old computer is on life support, and he clearly needs a new one. You watch as he tries to order a computer with his requests going backward and forward across literally five to seven different people and across at least three different departments. You see the calendar pages being torn off as the time lags on. You see the original employee struggling to make due with his old computer during the entire time. You see dollars being added to the cost of the computer all along the encumbered, old process. You see the employee so happy to finally see his new computer three months after he ordered it, only to tear his hair out when it doesn't work right. In contrast to this tragic tale, you see another cartoon in which the employee logs onto the company's intranet site created by Dell and properly configures her computer in ten minutes. An email with the requisition shows up on the boss's computer and is approved, and production begins automatically at one of Dell's factories. Three days later, the computer arrives at the employee's desk preconfigured and ready to go. The final scene in the cartoon shows a flow diagram of all the steps and time involved in the old system, contrasted with the new approach and a cost savings of 25 percent! The contrast is presented in an engaging way that involves multiple senses and results in breaking through the first barrier of change: The customer sees the need.

However, we do not want to create the impression that an entertaining cartoon is the key to success in helping customers see the need to change. As is likely clear to most readers, Dell's new approach required significant changes for the customer and its employees. For example:

- The change required central purchasing within the customer organization to give up a fair amount of control over the requisition process. No longer would they have the power to review every employee's requisition and decide that employee's fate. Rather, once purchasing and IT had worked with Dell to determine the policies, guidelines, and rules governing what computer configurations would be allowed to which types of employees, they could no longer keep their hands on the steering wheel or gearshift, and feet on the brakes and gas to control every move that was made.
- Second, bosses had to respond quickly (within 24 hours) or have their boss know they had not.
- Third, purchasing departments had to give up playing control cop over the generation of POs.
- Fourth, customers had to install software that would link them so tightly to Dell that Dell could see into and begin to recognize patterns in the customers' demand function for computers and software.

Customers resisted the change in part because they all had entrenched maps that had worked in the past. Perhaps most importantly for Dell, these maps were built on the premise that you never let your supplier see your demand function. The operating premise for most customers was: "As customers we tell suppliers like Dell what we need, not the reverse." To help customers see the need for this change, Dell had to work hard to help customers recognize the cost savings that could come from significantly fewer people handling paper. Dell had to focus on the increased accuracy that also came from fewer manual transcriptions of requisitions to PO to orders to computers. It had to help customers see the productivity benefits of getting employees on their computers in 3 versus 36 days. Ultimately, Dell had to help customers see that these and other benefits were greater than the monetary investments involved and the psychological and political pain of the change.

The critical point here is that breaking through this first barrier is not just an intellectual exercise. It is not usually sufficient to simply present some bullet points of the benefits of the change. It is necessary to illustrate the contrast between the old and the new in a way that engages multiple senses so that the contrast is compelling. Dell's example illustrates that the principles associated with breaking through the first barrier and helping people see the need for change not only apply to the context of customers but are actually more relevant with customers. Why? Because unlike employees, where if necessary one can leverage hierarchy and authority, when working with customers you can only leverage influence. It is pretty hard to tell a customer he must change or be fired.

As difficult as breaking through the first barrier is and as hard as it is to help the customer see the need for the change, Dell still had to break through Barrier #2 and help customers make the move. Because most customers had a well-established manual requisition and PO process, the first obstacle to the transition from doing the right thing poorly to doing it well was software. Each customer, in most cases, had its own proprietary software for keeping track of requisitions, POs, and deliveries. To make matters worse, customers often had different systems for each of these three major functions within their organizations, and many had different systems across different business units. Dell had to show customers that its software from WebMethods was the resource they needed to integrate effectively. Dell showed customers that because its software was built on open and uniform Internet standards, it could effectively interface with any customer's internal systems.

Even after customers took the plunge and made all the changes, Dell made sure that customers did not get tired or lost and consequently fail to finish. To ensure that customers did not get tired, Dell had dedicated champions assigned to each customer. Especially early on as the customer came online with the system, it was the champion's job to provide encouragement to customers. One of the key messages to customers was that their efforts were putting them at the cutting edge, and as a consequence would leave their competitors in the dust. This appeal to pride and sense of competition was quite motivating for customers, and kept them fighting through the inevitable glitches and problems of early trials.

Dell also made sure that customers did not feel lost. Dell monitored the results of the change and charted progress. It made sure that the results (good, bad, and ugly) were communicated on a regular basis to customers. Dell reported measures of accuracy, order fulfillment time, and estimated cost savings. As the customer saw the increase in these benefits, sponsors within the customer's organization could continue to fan the flames of motivation and enthusiasm for the change, pushing it to the point where it was well established and clearly successful. For these efforts, customers never got a chance to feel lost or give up. They knew where they were and what progress they were making on a monthly and sometimes weekly basis.

Dell's efforts to get its own suppliers to change and embrace the new vision were equally challenging. While Dell had more leverage over suppliers to get their buy-in to the vision, the criticality of suppliers effectively and efficiently implementing the change was no less daunting or important.

Suppliers had well-established mental maps that included features such as efficiencies derived from economies of scale in manufacturing and shipping. Suppliers were used to bidding on and winning large orders from Dell, which they would then produce and ship in large volumes. Furthermore, because these suppliers also had other customers, they had developed internal processes for allocating product and prioritizing customers when demand outstripped their internal capacity for supply.

Dell's vision for suppliers was nearly 180 degrees in the opposite direction of these proven, well-used maps. Dell's vision for suppliers had several key points:

- First, Dell would download orders every hour and generate a new manufacturing schedule every two hours that would reflect changes in job runs and priorities as well as components available.

- Second, suppliers would need to tie into Dell's system so intimately that suppliers would have only *15 minutes* to confirm an order placed by Dell.
- Third, once the order was confirmed, the supplier would then have *75 minutes* to get the order to Dell's factory. This meant that suppliers would have to locate warehouses physically near the Dell factory that they would supply. Dell's vision required that suppliers keep two weeks' worth of inventory in these close-by mini-warehouses.

Although Dell was one of the biggest customers, if not the biggest, for many of these suppliers and was the fastest-growing PC manufacturer, many suppliers were reluctant to make the required changes. Suppliers' mental maps of the past did not allow customers to see into their capacity, yet the nature of Dell's proposed integrated system would allow just that. For example, Dell cites the example of experiencing an up-tick in demand for a specific component, looking in to its supply chain and finding that one supplier had surplus capacity in one of its offshore factories. Dell then requested that the supplier use that capacity to meet the increased demand. To be clear, Dell did not ask the supplier if or how they could meet this up-tick in demand, but told the supplier it could, as well as where and how.

While Dell always had the bullet of "firing" a supplier if the supplier did not go along with this vision, Dell did not want to start what would become an intimate relationship with a shotgun marriage proposal. Instead, Dell focused on helping suppliers see the need for the new vision. By tying into the Dell system, suppliers would increasingly have a stable future. It was costly for both parties to become so intimately entwined and therefore equally difficult to divorce. By focusing on real-time manufacturing needs, both Dell and its suppliers could reduce inventories. Dell's objective was to go from two weeks to two hours of component inventory. Suppliers could in turn go from two months to two weeks of finished component inventory for Dell. Both could then enjoy the benefits of lower working capital and higher cash flow.

Like customers, even if suppliers bought into the vision, they still needed to believe in a path that could help them move from doing the right thing poorly to doing it well. In the case of suppliers, it was once again software that was the key resource for this path. Dell's software supplier for this part of the vision was i2 Technologies. This software lets suppliers see moment-by-moment demand within Dell for its products and lets Dell see into suppliers' capacity. While Dell expected this to increase velocity and save $150 million within the first five years, it achieved the savings within the first two years.

With such tight tolerances, any hiccup by any supplier had the potential to cause serious damage to the overall system. With only a two-hour inventory, most suppliers had to deliver several times per day. One missed delivery could shut down the factory.

Consequently, Dell could not afford for a supplier to get tired or lost and thereby fail to finish. As with customers, Dell assigned champions to every major supplier at the beginning to encourage them each step of the way. These champions played the role of both technical problem-solver, and more importantly of emotional cheerleader. To ensure that suppliers did not get lost, Dell monitored delivery performance constantly. Dell provided both positive and negative feedback about progress. Dell sent out detailed performance reports every month to suppliers to ensure that suppliers knew exactly how they had done compared to the past, as well as where their performance placed them relative to other suppliers. If a shipment was late by even a few minutes, Dell generated an instant written (electronic) reprimand. With so much feedback, suppliers had little chance of getting lost.

As mentioned earlier, Dell does not break out the financial performance of specific factories, but the evidence does suggest that these changes made with customers and suppliers generated significant effects. On the revenue side, the change created cost savings and productivity increases for customers. As a consequence, even at prices similar to competitors, Dell offered a better value proposition to customers, and as a consequence saw its market share steadily increase with corporate customers every year for four years after it implemented this change. In addition, the change increased customers' switching costs, which further reinforced repeat business with these customers. On the cost side, these changes contributed significant savings, such as the initial $150 million already mentioned.

Most readers will note that in 2006, Dell had a number of problems, especially regarding overheating batteries supplied by Sony. However, our point is not that Dell manages everything perfectly or that some company that mismanages a particular change is in general terrible. Clearly the problems Dell experienced in 2006 hurt the company's financial performance and shareholder value. However, it is worth speculating what the impact of these events might have been had the changes described earlier relative to customers and suppliers not already been effectively put in place.

Making Change Personal

Up to this point, we have focused on change by looking out at changing others—bosses, employees, customers, and suppliers. As we noted at the very outset of this book, rarely does a significant change in others require no change in the person leading that strategic change. From our experience in working with hundreds of senior executives and middle managers over the years, it seems that as difficult as it is to bring about change in others, it is at least as difficult, if not more difficult, to lead change in ourselves. As a consequence, in the last section of this chapter in which we wanted to pull the three aspects of change together, we thought it would be appropriate to make leading strategic change personal by examining the change journey of one individual.

This individual is the CEO of a medium-sized industrial company of about 6,000 employees. The company is integrated along the value chain in that it extracts raw materials, processes and manufactures them into products, and then sells those products both into wholesale channels as well as into its own retail channels. Approximately ten years ago, the company was less than half its current size and only one-tenth its current market value.

Like many companies, this one had success for several years by allowing the different business units a reasonable amount of autonomy. This approach not only fit the business environment of the time, but also fit the CEO's personal leadership style. While he understood the various businesses within the company, he preferred to let the business leaders pursue their individual unit goals. This enabled the CEO to work with each unit leader without having to truly build an executive team and deal with the challenges and conflicts that inevitably come with true integration.

While this description may make the CEO sound like he was not doing his job of building an executive team, it is important to appreciate two critical issues:

● First, this approach had yielded significant performance for the company. Over a 7-year period, the company out performed its competitors by a factor of 3.

● Second, the CEO was relatively young, and therefore no one (including members of the board of directors) put any pressure on him to build a team or look at grooming a successor.

Two things conspired against this wonderful and successful picture and past approach. First, as the company grew sufficiently in size, the cost of the duplication of resources and multiplication of different systems across the different business units increased to the point that the absolute dollars they represented could not be ignored. For example, while the company was small having separate IT systems and people for each business unit did not create significant duplication costs; however, by the time the company had 4,000 employees instead of 2,000, the duplication costs reached beyond $100 million—too big to ignore. Also, while 4 different payroll systems were costly to operate and support 7 years earlier, running 12 different systems and integrating them each year for company salary increase and bonus decisions was complex enough that the costs of running and integrating the current 12 systems cost 5 times that of the 4 past systems. The second major factor that conspired against continuing with the status quo was the increase in competition. Whereas before these extra expenses never mattered, now with increased competition and lower pricing power, un-captured cost savings were a key differentiator between good and great performance. If the company were to continue to outperform its peers, it would have to integrate both its business operations and its functional operations (such as IT, HR, maintenance, purchasing, and finance) more effectively and capture all the cost savings from economies of scale and simplicity.

After a series of strategy discussions and a workshop, the needed company change was clear to the CEO. However, one of the personal implications and needed changes was less clear. Integrating business units and functional activities would require integrating the executives who ran those units. This would necessitate a change in how the team operated, but most importantly it would require a change in how the CEO operated the team. The CEO would need to move from his normal style of working separately with each executive that reported to him to working more collectively with the team. In addition, team members would need to work more directly with each other. Figure 8.5 provides a visual illustration of this change.

The implications of this change were far greater than they seemed to the CEO at first. For example, in the past because each unit had autonomy and its own support functions, there was little need to resolve differences of opinion about the best performance management system or IT platform on which it should be run (PeopleSoft versus SAP). The new strategy required that these differences get worked out and agreed to so that an integrated and consequently a more efficient and effective system could be utilized.

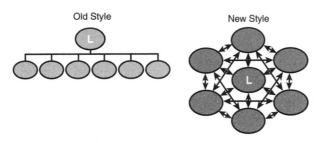

Figure 8.5 Change in team style.

While there had been differences of opinion in the past and even conflicts, the past structure and the CEO's approach allowed him to work things out not in a team setting but in one-on-one conversations. As we already mentioned, this one-on-one approach didn't just fit the old strategy and structure, but it fit the CEO's personality. He didn't like open confrontation or conflict in general and disliked it in a group setting in particular. Here it is important to appreciate that this was just one of several personal changes the change in strategy and structure would require of the CEO.

As simple as this might sound, most people, including the CEO of this company, are not infinitely flexible. They often build up behavior patterns not just because those behaviors are dictated by the environment, but because they fit personal preferences, biases, tendencies, innate proclivities, and the like. When these are then reinforced by success, they create a rather formidable barrier one must break through in order to change.

So in this case, how do you create the need for personal change? Clearly, if the needed business changes are not implemented because the CEO does not implement the needed personal changes, business results may deteriorate. If they deteriorate enough in either absolute or relative terms, then pressure will mount to push for the needed personal change. In fact, if the CEO waits long enough, things may deteriorate to the point that a crisis ensues and personal change is nearly unavoidable. Typically waiting until this point is very costly for all concerned. The crisis may result in financial losses that lead to layoffs, as well as declines in the stock price that hurt shareholder value. If shareholder losses are large enough, the CEO may find him or herself involuntarily headed for the exit as well—to join the laid-off employees.

So what can be done short of letting things drift into crisis to help the CEO see the need for personal change? Because there is no *one* right answer, we have to return to the fundamental principles we discussed relative to breaking through the first barrier of change. To help the CEO see the need for personal change, he needs a compelling contrast; he needs to see what is and what ought to be in a way that engages multiple senses. As we already stated, there is no single silver bullet, and often the actual solution requires multiple actions, not just one, to help someone see the need for personal change.

In this case, the external consultant working with the CEO determined that this particular CEO, with his engineering background, would need some data. As a consequence, 360 pieces of survey and interview data were gathered from the CEO's direct reports, as well as subordinates one level removed, and from board members. The written and interview questions focused primarily on the functionality and cohesiveness of the executive team. Whereas the CEO thought the team was great because he personally had a good and effective relationship with each member, others looked at the team not as a collection of CEO-direct report dyads, but as a whole group. When they looked at the group overall, they saw them as very uncoordinated and not aligned with each other. In fact, down in the ranks, people reported hearing members of the executive team (who reported to the CEO) complain about and cut down each other. In the extreme case, employees reported that they had heard their unit executive state that much of their unit's success and the past success of the company overall was due to the fact that *their* unit did not have to go along with the "dumb" approaches and decisions made by some of the other units and corporate functions.

These survey and interview data were in sharp contrast to the individual assessments of the CEO by his direct reports. Each direct report of the CEO respected him and loved working with him. As a consequence, they sent positive signals to the CEO, and not surprisingly, he felt based on these reinforcements that his one-on-one approach was a good one and was working well. Because he got on well with each executive on his team, in his mind he had an effective executive team.

Despite the fact that the survey and interview data painted a different picture, simply presenting the data to the CEO would not likely have the desired "breakthrough" effect. Why? Numbers are naturally one-dimensional. You can see them, but that is about it; it's hard to hear, taste, smell, or touch numbers. So what do you do? It would be great to show video recordings of the interviews and focus group sessions. The sensory impact of what was said and how things were said in these sessions would be powerful. However, policies of confidentiality precluded this as an option. So what do you do to create the contrast in a compelling way?

In this case, the consultant took the approach of first softening up the CEO by having him read a book entitled *The Five Dysfunctions of Teams*. Normally a book (especially a business book) is not a multi-sensory stimulus and therefore is not an effective means of creating compelling contrast. However in this case, the book selected was written more as a novel and much less as a list of the five ways to build executive teams. Just as literature novels can stimulate in our mind's eye images, sounds, smells, and the like, this "novel" about an executive building her team did the same. As a consequence, the contrast between running a team by focusing on individual dyads and building an integrated team became much clearer to the CEO.

This set the context and made the CEO much more receptive to his specific survey and interview data. Providing the data second in this simple sequence of actions gave them much more impact than they ever could have had presenting them first and on their own. After reviewing the data with the consultant, the CEO was convinced that his approach to the team needed to change in order for the change in company strategy and structure to be effective.

Among the various specific personal changes, managing conflict in a team setting was one of the most daunting for the CEO. With the help of a bit more data from a conflict style assessment instrument, the CEO recognized that he did not like open conflict and often sought to avoid conflict rather than confront the source of it.

With a bit more diagnosis, it was clear to the CEO that there were two fundamental drivers of this tendency to avoid conflict. First, the CEO had a general view that conflict was bad. Second, when conflict could not be resolved, especially in an open team setting, it often meant that the CEO would need to make a decision. His decisions, of course, would create "winners" and "losers." The CEO feared that this would simply create more tension and conflict in the future, as executives struggled and fought to ensure that they were on the "winning side" of the CEO's decisions the next time.

Most of these worries were reinforced by the fact that the CEO had relatively poor conflict management skills in the context of a group setting. The CEO was good at sitting down one-on-one with people and listening to their points of view and sharing his. In the cases where his view was contrary to that person's opinion or perspective, the CEO was reasonably good at helping the person appreciate his view and decision and getting that person on board. These skills seemed to abandon the CEO in a group setting. As a consequence, even though the CEO now recognized the need to change his personal behavior, he was reluctant to move because, like any of us, he had some preference for being competent rather than incompetent, even if being competent at managing team members one-on-one was not so right for the new integrated strategy and structure.

As a consequence, the CEO needed to better understand what was required to manage disagreements in a team setting and develop the associated skills. Only when he saw a path that would lead him from doing the new right thing poorly to doing it well would he be motivated to make this personal change. Working with an external executive coach, the CEO began the journey to develop the needed capabilities.

For example, a simple skill he worked on enhancing was that of establishing decision objectives before jumping into debates. In the past, the CEO had simply let people express their opinions straight out of the gate in meetings. When people disagreed (as they often did), this simply hardened each executive's position, making compromises or adjustments nearly impossible. In contrast, by taking time at the beginning of a discussion to establish what the key objectives were, the team could focus on how to meet the objectives rather than how to win their particular point of view.

As another example, the CEO himself was reasonably good at reflective listening, but not very good at getting this behavior out of others. In other words, the CEO was good at saying, "So, John do I understand that your main worry is X?" thereby ensuring that he had understood

John. As simple a change as it might seem, for the CEO to build a cohesive team, he needed all the members of the team to be skilled at reflective listening, and most importantly to feel it was their responsibility (not just the CEO's) to demonstrate this behavior. As a consequence, the CEO needed to work on not just exhibiting reflective listening himself, but getting others to exhibit the behavior. For example, instead of saying, "So, John do I understand that your main worry is X?" he needed to switch to more often asking questions that led others into reflective listening, such as "Before we get too far into this debate, Joe, can you summarize what John's main worry is?"

Clearly a few changes of wording are not the magic tricks that miraculously manage the team conflicts. Further, the effective management of the team's conflicts alone is not going to turn this unconnected executive team into a cohesive and integrated one overnight. The main point is that even though the CEO was 100 percent behind the needed organizational changes, achieving them required some personal change. These personal changes required first seeing the need and then making some specific personal moves. These moves were initiated by having a clear idea of the intended target (for example, managing team conflict) and developing certain skills and capabilities needed to hit that target.

As important as breaking through these first two barriers were, the CEO easily could have slipped back in the well-established and completely mastered past behaviors unless he had a clear plan of how to follow through to the finish. In this case, the CEO decided to have the HR executive on his team provide periodic feedback on how he was doing in terms of his targeted new behaviors. For example, after each executive committee meeting, the HR executive would provide her perspective on where the CEO did or did not establish objectives before diving into debates and where the CEO did or did not push the burden of reflective listening onto team members versus bearing it all himself. The follow-through plan also involved surveying and interviewing the same 360 individuals as participated in the first round six months later. Finally, the consultant reviewed the progress with the CEO about every two months. While there were other follow-up activities as well, these three went a very long way to ensuring that the CEO did not get tired or lost in a personal change process—a change process that took six months before it was solidly in place.

Summary

Clearly there is much more involved in the examples we have presented, and in any live cases you encounter, than we could explore in this book. Pulling all three elements of change—See, Move, Finish—together is easier said than done; but hopefully we have illustrated that the three barriers and the three principles for breakthrough change can be successfully applied to yourself or others, whether those others are above or below you, inside the company or outside the company.

Figure 8.6 provides a simple tool we often use to get an overall perspective on a change initiative relative to all three elements of the change model. To be clear, this tool is a stimulus for analysis, not a substitute for deeper diagnosis. When we use this tool, we typically have key agents in the change process complete it based on their "best guess" or sense of the situation. However, whenever possible we have found significant benefits of testing these estimates against actual sentiments from others (especially those most affected by the impending change). We have also used the tool as a means for conducting post-mortems on change projects to better understand what went right and wrong. This simple exercise can substantially increase the lessons learned and the value of those lessons for the next change challenge that is invariably lurking just around the corner ready to grab us.

Change Assessment
Instructions

Select a change initiative to assess. It is best to select a change initiative that you are currently facing or will soon face.

Once you have the change initiative in mind, simply follow the step-by-step assessment instructions based on the See, Move, Finish change model.

For each of the following statements, indicate the extent to which you agree or disagree by circling the appropriate number to the right. In responding to each item, use as a reference group those people who will be most directly and significantly impacted by the change initiative you have in mind. The reference group might be as small as a team or as large as all the employees in the company. Whatever is the case, simply use that group as your reference as you respond to the following statements.

See	1 Strongly Disagree	2 Disagree	3 Somewhat Disagree	4 Somewhat Agree	5 Agree	6 Strongly Agree
1. The contrast between where we are and where we need to be is clear.	Strongly Disagree	Disagree	Somewhat Disagree	Somewhat Agree	Agree	Strongly Agree
2. The reason for the needed change is clear to those most affected by it.	Strongly Disagree	Disagree	Somewhat Disagree	Somewhat Agree	Agree	Strongly Agree
3. How things will be after the change is clear—people can envision the destination.	Strongly Disagree	Disagree	Somewhat Disagree	Somewhat Agree	Agree	Strongly Agree
Move						
4. A powerful and capable team to lead the change is in place.	Strongly Disagree	Disagree	Somewhat Disagree	Somewhat Agree	Agree	Strongly Agree
5. Those who need to change understand the path forward.	Strongly Disagree	Disagree	Somewhat Disagree	Somewhat Agree	Agree	Strongly Agree
6. Those who need to change have the tools, resources, and capabilities to make the required changes.	Strongly Disagree	Disagree	Somewhat Disagree	Somewhat Agree	Agree	Strongly Agree
Finish						
7. Capable champions are in place who will reinforce early efforts and successes.	Strongly Disagree	Disagree	Somewhat Disagree	Somewhat Agree	Agree	Strongly Agree
8. Systems are in place to chart and communicate progress to individuals and groups.	Strongly Disagree	Disagree	Somewhat Disagree	Somewhat Agree	Agree	Strongly Agree
9. Key systems (e.g., rewards, performance appraisal, training, etc.) have been aligned to support (not work against) the required changes.	Strongly Disagree	Disagree	Somewhat Disagree	Somewhat Agree	Agree	Strongly Agree

Figure 8.6   Change assessment tool.

Now record your totals for each section by simply adding your scores:

See   (Q1 + Q2 + Q3) = _____

Move   (Q4 + Q5 + Q6) = _____

Finish   (Q7 + Q8 + Q9) = _____

Now add all three scores together:

TOTAL   = _____

Use the following table for a rough interpretation of your scores:

	3-8 pts Bad News	8-12 pts Not Good News	13-15 pts Good News	16-18 pts Great News
SEE	Change initiatives with these scores tend to fail on the launch pad. If they do get off the pad, they tend to come crashing back to earth.	Change initiatives with these scores tend to get started but then fizzle and fade.	Scores in this range often indicate enough fuel to get off the launch pad; but the change may lose momentum breaking through the first barrier.	Scores in this range often indicate enough fuel to get off the launch pad and make it successfully through the first barrier.
MOVE	Change initiatives with these scores (if they make it through the first barrier) slam to a stop at the second.	Change initiatives with these scores (if they make it through the first barrier), sputter but usually die before making it through the second barrier.	Scores in this range often signal enough momentum to push the envelope of the second barrier but tend to break through only for small to moderate change initiatives.	Scores in this range usually lead to success in breaking through the second barrier.
FINISH	Scores in this range occur even when scores for See and Move are high. Unfortunately, with scores in this range the change initiative still is likely to be among the 70% that ultimately fail.	Scores in this range suggest that while the change might achieve initial success, it will fall far short of its goal and has a high chance of ultimate failure.	If the scores for See and Move were high, there's hope, but if they were only good, this is likely to be the end—with the designation in sight but just out of reach.	While nothing is guaranteed, scores in this range in combination with strong See and Move scores put you in the elite group whose change initiative likely succeeds.
TOTAL	9-24 pts Bad News	25-37 pts Not Good News	38-47 pts Good News	48-54 pts Great News
	The odds of your change initiative succeeding are as good as a motorcycle breaking through a thick, concrete wall.	You may feel like you've got the odds of success on your side, but you don't. You have a 70% chance of failure.	You're close enough that if there's time you can strengthen some aspects of the change initiative and still succeed.	With total scores in this range, the odds are on your side. You have a better than 70% chance of success.

Figure 8.6   Change assessment tool (continued).

Which if the three general areas of See, and Move, and Finish had the lowest scores (✓ one of the following)?

See _____

Move _____

Finish _____

What are the three biggest reasons that explain this area of weakness? In answering this question, do not stop at a superficial level, but dig deep. For example, if a particular muscle group is weak, the superficial explanation might be "It wasn't exercised enough." Greater insight comes from asking, "Why wasn't this muscle group exercised more?" Take a similar probing approach in explaining why the weakest area is (was) weak.

1. _____

2. _____

3. _____

With a clear idea of what area is (was) weakest and why, now think about corrective actions. What three high-impact actions do you need to take (or should have been taken if you are assessing a past change) in order to bring this previously marked area of weakness up to a level of strength?

1. _____

2. _____

3. _____

If you undertook these actions, how would your responses and scores for the items in the survey on the first page change? How much would your score for that area improve?

Would it move into the "Good New" level? How would this specific change in score change your total score? Would it move you into at least the "Good News" level overall?

Figure 8.6 Change assessment tool (continued).

As we have stressed throughout this book, we are not trying to provide a comprehensive road map with every little highway or byway on it. Both research and practice lead us to believe that while exhaustiveness can make for long and complete books, it makes for short-lived and unsuccessful practice. People use what they remember, not what they read. For most of us, that means we remember between 13 and 25 percent of what we read. That is why we have focused on the core 20 percent of change barriers and principles that will get you 80 percent of the way to your desired result.

With this fundamental principle in mind, in the last chapter, we highlight some of the unique challenges and benefits of anticipatory change versus reactive change—or waiting until there is a crisis demanding change.

Getting Ahead of the Change Curve

Leading strategic change is not just about leading big and important changes, but it is also about leading change that helps create and sustain competitive advantage. This requires not only understanding the three barriers to successful change, but also appreciating three fundamental types of change—anticipatory, reactive, and crisis.

Anticipatory change is just that anticipating the strategic need for change rather than waiting for it to show up at your front door. In other words, anticipatory change demands that we look ahead over the horizon and around the corner to see in advance the signs that indicate change might be needed—in ourselves and in our organizations. This approach requires us to recognize early, long before irrefutable evidence accumulates, that our old, right map may soon become wrong. Based on this determination, the subsequent challenge is to figure out what the new right map should be in the face of some uncertainty and to get others to see the need for change while it is still far off in the distance.

Reactive change is where most of us spend most of our time. This approach revolves around reacting to obvious signs and signals that change is needed. These signs and signals surface from customers, competitors, technology, shareholders, employees, and other critical stakeholders warning us that we should change today or pay for our delay with a heavier price tomorrow.

When we fail to look out the window to see anticipatory change opportunities, when we ignore the knock on the door signaling the need for reactive change, *crisis change* comes crashing in our nice orderly house and we are forced to deal with it or die.

Whether you've used these three labels or not, you have no doubt seen all three types of change. When asked which of these three types of changes is the most difficult, often people will instinctively say "crisis change." In actuality, crisis change is the least difficult of the three types of change to get going. After all, when you are truly in a crisis and many customers have abandoned you, credit agencies have given you a low junk rating, suppliers have put you on cash payment terms, and the smell of bankruptcy is in the air, it is easier to get people moving than when the sun is shining and things are going well, when the signals for change are far off in the distance they are both hard to see and harder still to convince others what the right change is or that movement in that direction is needed now. When placed in this light, most managers agree that anticipatory change is actually the most difficult (see Figure 9.1). However, when you think about the cost of change, crisis change is clearly the most costly. Once you drift into crisis and need to lay off half your employees and rack up poor financial performance that cost your shareholders half their value, the cost of crisis change becomes all too real.

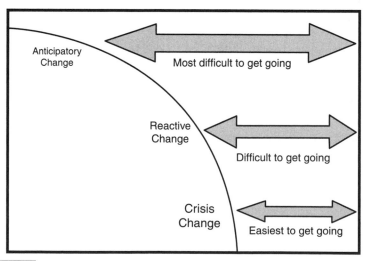

Figure 9.1 The difficulty of change.

Because anticipatory change is difficult, most of us wait and end up sliding down the slippery slope of the change curve from anticipation to reactionary and finally bottom out at crisis. As we do, the costs of change grow, and typically they grow exponentially (see Figure 9.2).

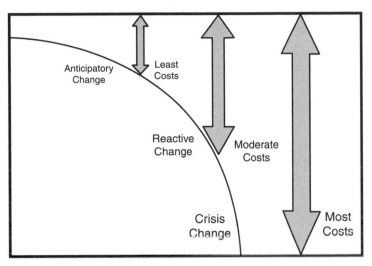

Figure 9.2   The costs of change.

If you were to superimpose Figure 9.1 on Figure 9.2, you could see that the difficulty and costs of change along these three types of change—anticipatory, reactive, and crisis—are inversely related to each other. As difficulty of change increases, costs of change decline. Conversely, as costs increase, difficulty declines. To see why this is the case, let's dig below the surface on this powerful dynamic by starting with the last approach first—crisis change.

Crisis Change

While certainly not the only culprit, success can often be the mother of crisis change. For example, Nissan had such a strong period of growth for more than 20 years that executives ignored the signals of needed change for so long that a foreign partner, Renault, and foreign leader, Carlos Goshen, was brought in to manage the crisis. Likewise, Kmart grew successfully for decades and ignored changes in customers and competitors until the crisis forced it into the unflattering title of the biggest retail bankruptcy in U.S. history.

Xerox enjoyed such success that the name of the company became a common use verb for the process it pioneered—as in "Please xerox (copy) this for me." In 1999, Rick Thoman from IBM, who by all accounts was quite capable and successful in the past, was brought in to lead the company out of crisis. Yet Thoman lasted less than two years at the helm. Facing an even deeper crisis and continued losses in the tens of millions of dollars, in 2001 Xerox promoted one of their own, Anne Mulcahy, to CEO to try and turn things around.

While Carlos Goshen was successful with getting Nissan out of the crisis, Rick Thoman was not. When you think about these and many other examples, it is clear that leading "crisis change" is not simply a walk in the park. If you start from a deep enough hole and enough customers have abandoned you and most of your competition have left you in their dust, recovering can be a daunting challenge. But in terms of getting change going, crisis change is easier than anticipatory change. After all, how hard is it to convince people that the old map is now wrong when your credit rating is downgraded monthly, when losses mount daily, and when your stock price falls hourly? Also, how precise do the required changes in a crisis need to be? For example, if labor costs are excessive, how hard is it to cut one-third of your workforce? How much precision does that really take? It may require a strong stomach, but how much skill is required to tell every third person that they are fired?

As an analogy for this corporate situation, compare the worlds of a battlefield medic and vascular surgeon. How much training does a battlefield medic need compared to a vascular surgeon? A battlefield medic's training is measured in months, while a vascular surgeon's is measured in years. Why? Imagine yourself on the battlefield where someone's arm is shattered by an explosion. Bullets are whizzing overhead. The enemy is advancing. What do you do? You are clearly in a crisis. You can't take time to try and carefully patch the arm back together. No, you put a tourniquet on the arm to stop the bleeding, and fast! Perhaps the soldier loses the arm. Maybe you have to cut off the arm to save the person. There isn't time for precision; you're in a crisis. Maybe you should have cut it off an inch higher or lower than you did, but there's no time to worry about that. Indeed, if you had the time and were not in a crisis, then, as a vascular surgeon, you could perform the seven-hour operation to restore the torn muscles, reconnect the severed blood vessels, and save the arm.

Please don't misunderstand us. We are not suggesting that anyone can become a battlefield medic or that anyone can perform a successful company turnaround. However, we are saying that the inherent nature of crisis change makes it much easier to break through the failure to see barrier as well as the failure to move barrier in comparison to anticipatory change. After all, if you don't see or move when a crisis hits, you are as good as dead.

However, just as the battlefield crisis results in greater blood, suffering, and loss of life or limb, so too does crisis change in a company or in a person's career. Crisis change almost always costs money, shareholder value, customer loyalty, and the livelihoods of many employees. Thus, while crisis change is the easiest of the three to initiate, it is also the most costly for almost everyone affected by it.

Reactive Change

Reactive change is the most common approach we see in organizations. Reactive change is harder to get going than crisis change because less evidence exists that the successful map of the past is indeed wrong for the future. It is typically less costly than crisis change because it usually happens before the red ink flows freely and the workforce must be cut in half for sheer survival. Take notice, though—we do not want to create the impression that reactive change is bad per se. The more uncertain the signs and signals that the business environment is shifting, the more prudent it may be to wait and react. In fact, if you have established a general level of change agility within your organization, it may be much better to respond as a quick second mover instead of a first mover. However, the junk pile of derailed careers of leaders who were slow second movers is both high and wide. While a great temptation looms ever present for firms and individual leaders to drift down the slippery slope from anticipatory to reactive change, we should remember and count the very real costs and consequences of failing to pull off anticipatory change.

Anticipatory Change

Everyone knows from experience that anticipatory change is very hard—especially initially. Just as it is difficult to see physical objects when they are far off in the distance, so too is it hard to help people sense business threats or opportunities when they are either on or sometimes over the visible horizon. Furthermore, even if we do help others see these distant threats or opportunities, the farther away they are, the greater the chance that they can change course, and as a consequence, what we thought was the required anticipatory change may not be completely right. In fact, this is often the rationale managers give for not leading anticipatory change.

We all understand these related dynamics, and so we are, with good reason, nervous about the time, energy, money, and other valuable investments that might be wasted in off-target anticipatory change. This type of thinking is only reinforced the longer and more successful our personal or business mental maps have been.

To be sure, we are not advocating reckless or thoughtless anticipatory change. However, it is important to remind ourselves of the potential benefits and low costs of insightful anticipatory change when executed correctly. The principles and benefits we want to highlight can accrue not just to organizations, but to individual managers as well.

The first fact to keep in mind at an individual and organization level is: Because anticipatory change is difficult, generally the demand for capable anticipatory change leaders exceeds the supply. Any basic economics course teaches that when demand exceeds supply, prices rise. Premiums are paid when demand outstrips supply, whether those premiums are paid in terms of career advancement to individuals or in higher share prices to companies. To the extent, as we argued in Chapter 1, "The Challenge of Leading Strategic Change," that the speed and uncertainty of change is increasing, anticipatory change will be evermore challenging, and as a consequence we can reasonably predict that a shortage of anticipatory change leaders will continue. As it does, first mover advantages will accrue to both companies and individuals that do not shy away from anticipatory change.

This is especially true when the change involves long and steep learning curves, though you might be inclined to conclude just the opposite. After all, long and steep learning curves (reflecting the significant amount of learning required to do the new right thing well) mean that the payoffs will not show up initially. This is precisely why many of us that start up the long and steep learning curve of a new language or musical instrument, give up before long—the results we desire and that would naturally reinforce our efforts just don't show up quickly enough. However, it is for precisely that reason that the sooner you get your company on the change curve, the greater your firm's advantage over slower changing competitors. As Figures 9.3 and 9.4 illustrate, for each equal interval of time during the learning process, once you get into the "fat" part of the learning curve, the greater

your advantage and the distance you put between yourself and
your competitors.

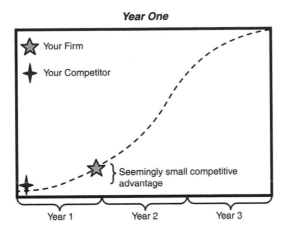

Figure 9.3   Moving fast and first up steep learning curves year one.

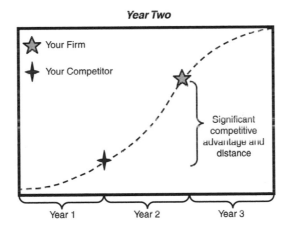

Figure 9.4   Moving fast and first up steep learning curves year two.

For example, consider the rivalry between Sony and Apple. Actually
before Apple's iPod, most executives at Sony would have not even
listed Apple as a key competitor. Theoretically, Sony should have won
this contest just as it won the earlier one in the 1980s with the Sony
Walkman. Sony had hardware and software, and owned one of the
largest music libraries and a stable of current popular singers and
groups. Yet, while Apple launched the iPod in 2001, Sony did not
respond with similar product until 2005. By then, Apple had more than

70 percent of the market share along with loyal and satisfied customers. The learning curves, especially in terms of the software that made the iPod so easy to use and getting multiple record labels to put their music on Apple's iTune online store, are long and steep. Even if Sony with its new foreign CEO, Howard Stringer, throws their best "mountain climbers" at these long and steep learning curves, it will take some time before they can catch up to Apple. No doubt, Apple's advantage will not last forever, but in today's competitive world, when you can enjoy a substantial advantage over a well-known company such as Sony for five or ten years, most of us would (and should) gladly take it.

We might also look at the rivalry between Pepsi and Coke in Vietnam (with its 80 million people). The learning curves for manufacturing, distributing, and selling beverages in Vietnam are also long and steep. Understanding and mastering the nuances of working effectively with a joint venture partner that was a former state-owned enterprise are difficult to say the least. Workers have to be hired and trained to focus not just on volume, but also on world-class quality. Because of the fractured nature of the market, literally dozens and dozens of relationships with distributors have to be formed to get your product to market. The retail shops for distribution to consumers are so fragmented that it takes literally thousands of relationships with mom and pop shops just to get your product out in the south of Vietnam. Now add to this the learning curves of marketing and advertising effectively in Vietnam and the fact that what it takes to sell your product in the U.S. will not necessarily get you the same results half way around the world. Hundreds of differences and pitfalls await you. For example, you have to be careful that your slogan, "Come alive with the new Pepsi generation," does not get mistakenly translated as "Pepsi will bring your ancestors back from the dead" (as it did in one of the Asian markets).

Do all the investments of anticipatory change and going after emerging markets to grow the company deliver results immediately? No. Coke follows Pepsi into Vietnam only by a year or two, and the distance between the two initially does not seem like much. However, as Pepsi entered into the fat part of the learning curve, the benefits of this anticipatory change became more evident. Today, Pepsi rules the economically vibrant southern part of Vietnam. Coke is taking refuge in the north. Will this advantage last forever? No. But as we already stressed, in this hyper-competitive world, an advantage of even a few years is one worth enjoying.

Change Penalty

We, of course, could cite lots of other examples of the triumphs and travails of companies that made anticipatory changes and those that drifted into crisis: Nokia and Motorola; WalMart and Kmart, Encyclopedia and Wikipedia, and so on. However, in fairness, it is important to point out that not only is there a period during anticipatory change when the anticipated results are slow to appear, but quite often there is a change penalty when, after moving onto the new learning curve, performance actually declines.

For us, one of the most poignant individual examples is Tiger Woods. Yes, Tiger Woods the golfer. Even those who don't care much for golf have undoubtedly heard of Tiger and his record performances ever since he turned professional in 1996. However, what is not quite as well-known are the two anticipatory changes he made *and* the penalties he paid. These are illustrated in Figure 9.5.

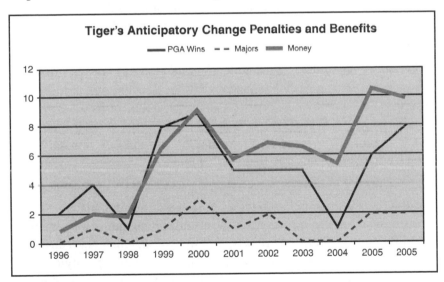

Figure 9.5 Tiger Woods' anticipatory change.

As Tiger came out of arguably one of the most successful amateur careers and enjoyed success enough to be named "Rookie of the Year," Tiger anticipated a needed change. According to Tiger, "People thought it was asinine for me to change my swing after I won the Masters by 12 shots. ... *Why would you want to change that?* Well, I thought I could become better."[1] His work with coach Butch Harmon soon proved

[1] "The Truth about Tiger," by Jaime Diaz, *Golf Digest*, January, 2005.

doubters wrong as he paid the price in 1998, but captured the benefits in 1999 and enjoyed what is arguably one of the best seasons by anyone in golf history in 2000.

However, even as his fortunes and successes—like his drives off the tee—were still outdistancing virtually all competitors, in 2003 he began changing his swing again. Once again people asked, "Why in the heck would he do that? How could the player who from 1999 to 2002 had produced arguably the greatest golf ever played want to change his swing?"[2] Once again with this change, he paid a change penalty. The penalty was in full force throughout 2004 and reached a rather visible point when he finished 33 strokes behind Phil Mickelson in the Masters. When asked at the end of one of his worst seasons since turning pro why he persisted in making what was clearly the wrong change, Tiger replied, "I'd like to play my best more frequently, and that's the whole idea. That's why you make changes. I thought I could become more consistent and play at a higher level more often. ... I've always taken risks to try to become a better golfer, and that's one of the things that has gotten me this far."[3]

What do we take from this example in golf and others we have seen in business? First, anticipatory change is not for the faint of heart. There are no free lunches, and with great desired reward comes commensurate risk. Anticipatory change requires the courage and eye of the *tiger*, as it were, in individual leaders and in a company's leadership team collectively.

Second, it also seems clear that a very high level of aspiration is required—aspiration not necessarily for fame or fortune, but for improvement and being one's best as an individual and as a company. The drive for extraordinary reliability, innovation, efficiency, capacity, quality, speed, beauty, comfort, convenience, durability, fit, style, taste, sound, smell, texture, and on and on are simply what is required to inspire people to step ahead of the rationale of risk. Without a passionate pursuit of the extraordinary, risks so typically and tightly tied to anticipatory change will likely win the day, and we will end up waiting and drifting down to reactionary change. However, the pursuit of the extraordinary need not require a priest's vow of isolation or poverty. As Tiger's example illustrates, in a free market environment

[2] Ibid.
[3] Ibid.

fame and fortune will ultimately shun mediocrity and seek out extraordinary performance.

Third, because, at best, positive results from anticipatory change do not show up quickly and because more often change penalties first emerge, it seems clear to us that commitment is an essential characteristic for successful anticipatory change. If we take on anticipatory change in ourselves or our units, we can help the process by informing others' expectations and explaining that the relationship between effort and results is not a linear one over time, but rather is curvilinear. While this is a helpful tactic, it will not likely eliminate the slings and arrows that will be flung our way during the early stage of anticipatory change when the change penalties rear their ugly heads. As a consequence, for anyone initiating anticipatory change, it seems there is little substitute for sheer commitment to press on.

Conclusion

Let's finish our journey through *It Starts with One* with a few final thoughts. First, even though we spent a good part of this final chapter on anticipatory change, it is not the only approach to change. Furthermore, none of us spend all our time in the world of anticipatory change. We may well slip unintentionally into reactive change or find ourselves thrust into a change crisis. To make sure there is no misunderstanding, the principles of *It Starts with One* work as well in reactive and crisis change settings as they do in anticipatory change situations.

Yet, we concluded this final chapter with a discussion of anticipatory change for a specific reason. Because anticipatory change is the most difficult, we should not be surprised that is where the supply of successful change leaders falls the shortest. Also, because anticipatory change is where the potential payoffs are the biggest, that is where demand for successful change leaders is and will forever be the greatest. From our extensive consulting work and research, the conclusion is clear: Anticipatory change leaders are in great demand and extremely short supply.

Demand outstripping supply is a very powerful reason for mastering the art and science of leading change. In this book, we have shared some proven principles of change that can help you break through the brain barriers of change and help yourself and others to see, move, and finish.

In previous chapters, we have supplied you with practical solutions and tools to become a master leader of strategic change at the personal, team, or organizational level. The key to breaking through the barriers to change lie not just in grasping the principles, but also applying them in practice.

To put these principles into practice, they have to become personal. To help illustrate this, consider the following. Hal's father was one of those old-time dads who could fix anything. To do this he studied the principles of electricity, mechanics, fluids, and construction. When it came time to fix a diesel engine, gasoline engine, or refrigerator motor, he was a master at putting the principles into practice. His shop was full of almost every tool you could imagine, and some you couldn't. The ones you couldn't imagine were those he created himself. Because he understood what needed to be fixed and how to fix it so well, when the right tool wasn't commercially available, he made it.

Similar to Hal's father, we hope that you not only take the challenge to master the principles and practices for breaking through change barriers (an endeavor that requires years, not months, to truly excel at), and that you will also become so adept at the craft of change that it will become second nature to create unique tools to meet the specific demands of your change initiatives.

To conclude the journey, let's go back to the beginning and as T.S. Eliot once put it, "Know the place for the first time." Lasting change starts from the inside out—by first changing individuals. In many cases, the first person to change is ourselves. We change individuals, ourselves and others, by remapping minds to see, move, and finish. By changing individuals, we really can change organizations.

Index

Ⅷ Wharton School Publishing

In the face of accelerating turbulence and change, business leaders and policy makers need new ways of thinking to sustain performance and growth.

Wharton School Publishing offers a trusted source for stimulating ideas from thought leaders who provide new mental models to address changes in strategy, management, and finance. We seek out authors from diverse disciplines with a profound understanding of change and its implications. We offer books and tools that help executives respond to the challenge of change.

Every book and management tool we publish meets quality standards set by The Wharton School of the University of Pennsylvania. Each title is reviewed by the Wharton School Publishing Editorial Board before being given Wharton's seal of approval. This ensures that Wharton publications are timely, relevant, important, conceptually sound or empirically based, and implementable.

To fit our readers' learning preferences, Wharton publications are available in multiple formats, including books, audio, and electronic.

To find out more about our books and management tools, visit us at whartonsp.com and Wharton's executive education site, exceed.wharton.upenn.edu.

Wharton
UNIVERSITY of PENNSYLVANIA